Are You Your Own Worst Enemy?

Are You Your Own Worst Enemy?

THE NINE INNER STRENGTHS YOU NEED
TO OVERCOME SELF-DEFEATING
TENDENCIES AT WORK

Charles E. Watson and Thomas A. Idinopulos

PRAEGER

Westport, Connecticut
London

Library of Congress Cataloging-in-Publication Data

Watson, Charles E.
 Are you your own worst enemy? : the nine inner strengths you need to
overcome self-defeating tendencies at work / Charles E. Watson and
Thomas A. Idinopulos.
  p. cm.
 Includes bibliographical references and index.
 ISBN 978–0–275–99224–8 (alk. paper)
 1. Organizational behavior. 2. Self-management (Psychology)
3. Responsibility. 4. Integrity. 5. Emotional intelligence.
6. Work—Psychological aspects. I. Idinopulos, Thomas A. II. Title.
III. Title: Overcome self-defeating tendencies at work.
 HD58.7.W332 2007
 650.1—dc22 2007020619

British Library Cataloguing in Publication Data is available.

Library of Congress Catalog Card Number: 2007020619
ISBN-13: 978–0–275–99224–8

First published in 2007

Praeger Publishers, 88 Post Road West, Westport, CT 06881
An imprint of Greenwood Publishing Group, Inc.
www.praeger.com

Printed in the United States of America

The paper used in this book complies with the
Permanent Paper Standard issued by the National
Information Standards Organization (Z39.48–1984).

10 9 8 7 6 5 4 3 2 1

CONTENTS

INTRODUCTION

Who doesn't want to perform admirably at work and enjoy an exciting career? We all want to move ahead and be rewarded for our accomplishments. We all want to develop our talents and skills and be respected. We'd also like to find meaning in our work. But today's fast-paced, highly competitive world of work is challenging. It isn't easy to make oneself into a superior performer. In truth, most people do not come anywhere near reaching their full potential when it comes to workplace effectiveness. Despite their best intentions and worthy efforts to improve themselves, many people fall short of being the superior performers they would like to be. They fall behind others who actually outperform them. They do not move ahead. They end up earning less money than they feel they are worth. Their jobs do not bring them the satisfaction they crave. What could be the difficulty? What holds people back from performing better in the workplace?

The truth is that from time to time everyone will stumble over some personal flaw and fall flat on his or her face. We are all vulnerable to self-defeating tendencies that can hurt us and hold us back. While others are the source of much of the pain and irritation we encounter at work, and while circumstances often conspire against us, it is we ourselves who are at the heart of our difficulties. Even the best of us will do things now and then that end up making us small, unproductive, dissatisfied. That's why we wrote this book: to show smart, capable, well-meaning people how their inner tendencies often lead to certain actions that make them their own worst enemies. But this book does not focus on problems alone. It contains practical advice in the form of concrete examples that illustrate methods all of us can follow to develop the inner strengths needed to overcome those foibles and frailties that defeat us in the workplace. We recognize the economic realities faced by working people, particularly single women who need an income to support a family. Most people are interested in earning more, which requires moving ahead to improve their economic situation. A word of caution is in order—this is not a guide for how to get rich. Following our advice will not guarantee material success, but it should lead you to become a better performer in the workplace.

To understand better what it is about certain assumptions, attitudes, and behaviors that make them limiting or downright destructive, we need to peer deeply into our human nature and consider more fully what it means to be effective, alive, and complete contributors in the workplace. We begin our explanation by considering the universe and the tiny space occupied in it by the earth. What should capture our special attention here is the fact that ours is the only planet where life is known to exist. Life may exist elsewhere and in other forms beyond our ability to comprehend, but as far as we know it does not. We gain an invaluable sense of humility and respect for our human situation when we recognize that we did not create this thing called life. We are part of the cosmos but not the center of it. Still, we are unique and a useful part of our universe. It is because of these simple realities that serious minds regard all life as precious, something of immense importance and the work of an awesome source of power and wonderment. If we truly reverence life we will try to understand what its possibilities are for ourselves.

Life for human beings involves far more than the physiological processes of breathing, blood circulation, digestion, and reproduction. Unlike lower life forms that exist and function in a seemingly preprogrammed way established by what we believe to be genetic coding and instinct, human life involves more than mere physiology. Humans also live on another level, in another dimension. They have both an outside and an inside—they can assimilate more than just molecules of oxygen and food; they can be changed by ideas and they can create ideas and objects. Whereas one bird or plant or fish or insect of a species is very much like the others of that species, we cannot say this of people. Each person is strikingly unique. Each person has a distinctive capacity for memory, self-consciousness, thoughtfulness, purposefulness, affection, and creative expression. The differences that exist between people arise not so much from what each is given in terms of physical endowments but from what each person does with his or her native abilities. While some of our uniqueness can be accounted for by our differing physiological attributes, most of it comes from what we make of ourselves, from how we choose to shape our whole personality.

It is worth noting that each human being is capable of doing well or poorly with his or her self. Humans have the power to make themselves into something admirable or allow themselves to degenerate into something despicable. Humans are unique in that they are the only living species with the capacity to act in both self-destructive and self-nurturing ways, whether physical, emotional, or spiritual. In other words, humans can choose to act in ways that make themselves either more or less fully human depending on how well they use or don't use their human capabilities, and whether they develop them or let them deteriorate. Whereas plants and animals develop into the creatures they were designed to become from birth, humans have the unique capacity and opportunity to shape themselves into the personalities they would like to become. These basic ideas lead to an important insight: We are self-creating creatures who work with what nature gives us and we shape ourselves into the persons we are capable of becoming.

In this book we examine patterns of workplace behavior by which people can injure themselves as persons. You will see how humans can sometimes act in ways that make themselves either less or more effective by what they believe and choose to do. We will present a basic framework for better understanding what it is that makes humans what they are, unique creatures with amazing powers of thinking and feeling, of choosing and creating, of loving and reverencing. The theme of our book is this: people become their own worst enemy whenever they refuse to accept their gifts of life—the dimensions that compose their humanity. We have come to the conclusion that there is only one way to accept these gifts of life completely and that is by acknowledging them, using them, and perfecting them to their fullest. We cease being our own worst enemy when we use and nurture our human endowments—our free will, our powers of thought, our ability to act, our capacity to love others, our creative impulses, our ability to improve, our willingness to work, and our capacity to be in awe of realities greater than ourselves—for the benefit of ourselves and others.

We are acutely aware of the fact that many humans behave in ways that harm their physical bodies. They can act in unsafe and unhealthful ways. The devastating effects that alcohol and illegal drug usage have on human lives and workplace productivity are well documented. The overall rate of drug abuse in America is 5 percent of the population—and two thirds of these people are employed. An estimated thirteen million Americans are alcoholics. The cost of alcohol and illicit drug abuse in the workplace is immense. The Substance Abuse and Mental Health Services Administration reported in 1995 that "alcohol and drug abuse costs U.S. businesses $102 billion annually in lost productivity, incidents and employee turnover." One study estimated that the chemically dependent employee is usually less than 75 percent effective. While we see the obvious—that people destroy their lives and diminish their performance in the workplace by substance abuse—our book does not deal with these issues. There are highly qualified people trained to deal with substance abuse problems and we seriously urge those with such problems to get the professional help they need. We are not qualified to speak on such matters beyond what we have just suggested. Our book deals not with substance abuse but with philosophical and psychological matters—how humans harm their uniquely human capacities.

Why is it that many people, perhaps most people, are at one time or another their own worst enemy? What is it that most keeps them from accepting, using, and developing their gifts of life, those qualities that make them truly human? Thoughtful observation will reveal the answer: they strive too hard to grasp those things which are commonly thought to be indicators of success—wealth, power, prestige. We see success as being something different. We define it as doing good things with whatever abilities a person has. This means mastering and thoughtfully using one's human capabilities for purposes that transcend oneself. We see success occurring when a person rises above the drive to obtain and feel safe and secure in material objects. The kind of success we are talking about goes beyond basking in feelings of smugness and importance from one's accomplishments and from having secured the approval of others for having outperformed everyone else. We see success as being the living of an authentic life, courageously struggling to do the best one can with his or her natural endowments in the circumstances he or she encounters. An unusually talented person with gifts of intellect and sharp wit may do better in terms of pay and rank than someone of only average intellect and verbal ability. Yet the latter person may actually struggle more gallantly with issues of right and wrong, be more authentic in interactions with others and more trustworthy because of it, and may come up with more creative approaches to bettering the quality of work, even if only in small ways, than their more gifted counterparts. We believe that what happens *within* us is more significant than what happens *to us*.

We believe that the key to effective performance in the workplace— and to lasting satisfaction with one's work—lies in fully awakening, using, and developing one's human capacities. This is particularly true in knowledge-based economies, such as ours, where people are paid to use their minds more than their backs. We also need to recognize that in every life there is to be found some flaw, some weakness, some appetite, or some disabling peculiarity that lurks ready to limit or harm or even destroy the person completely. We need to face our trouble-inviting foibles honestly and then either control them or work around them, or, better yet, learn to harness and use them to higher purposes. But we must never ignore our vulnerabilities or pretend that they don't exist. In this book we will point out the difficulties people face and struggle with—be they from circumstances in which they find themselves or from frailties within their own personalities—as they try to use and nurture their human capacities.

We see nine capacities that distinguish humans from all other life forms, nine essential elements that are uniquely human. These are the same elements that make people highly effective contributors in the workplace. The chapters of this book are organized accordingly.

1. *The capacity to rise above passivity, accept responsibility, and initiate action.* An effective person in the workplace acts responsibly, doing what ought to be done without having to be told exactly what to do in light of unfolding circumstances.
2. *The capacity for self-understanding and self-acceptance.* Each human is unique and it is important for each person to identify his or her unique interests and abilities, allowing them to influence their decisions in choosing work and doing things at work that best tap their special abilities and passions.
3. *The capacity to think and to dignify one's existence by high-quality thinking.* Thinking involves the ability to reason, to make informed judgments, to see beyond the obvious, to solve problems, to figure things out for oneself. Thinking liberates an individual, giving the person the capacity to engage the world as an active being, to make informed choices, and to advance knowledge for self and others to use.

4. *The capacity to respect persons, to treat others with kindness, and to be as concerned for their well-being as much as one is for her own.* A highly effective person in the workplace restrains her actions, treating others not as she might feel like treating them but as she knows she ought to treat them.

5. *The capacity to create.* Humans have a divine-like, inborn element in their makeup. It is the power to create. By using these creative powers, highly effective people are able to expand and perfect them.

6. *The capacity to expand one's knowledge and understanding; to learn and grow intellectually and emotionally.* Learning is not something one person can do for another person. It is something that a person must do for himself. The most effective people found in the workplace have the amazing ability to turn each experience into a powerful lesson, which is then used to guide thoughts and actions in the days ahead.

7. *The capacity to see and inspect one's behavior.* The ability to control oneself is the benefit one derives from this human capacity. Without this capacity, people would be unable to live by the virtues we all admire—qualities such as punctuality, industriousness, perseverance, civility, rules of etiquette.

8. *The capacity to distinguish between good and evil and to choose right from wrong.* We live in a world in which there exists a moral order. We make ourselves more secure, we earn the trust and respect of others, and we become more effective when we live by ethical standards, when we choose to act morally.

9. *The capacity to be of service to others.* Without the capacity to be in awe of powers and ideals that are greater than oneself and ideals that dignify life, humans would behave as though they were gods. They would make themselves petty-minded and would diminish and destroy themselves because of it. Having a sense of awe for things like truth, beauty, justice, goodness, God—the ideals and powers that ennoble the quality of life on our planet, inspire humans to want to serve worthy ends, which ultimately give their lives meaning and dignity.

The ideal for anyone is to become a complete person by using and developing his or her capacities to their fullest. But reaching this ideal, as we all know, is never easy. This is because we are vulnerable to the ill effects of our own inner tendencies that keep us from bringing the full possibilities of our personhood to bear on our work. In addition, outside forces and circumstances often work against us: unfairness, pettiness, misfortune, tragedy, malice. Indeed, our world is not as generous and evenhanded in its treatment of people as we might think the Creator would want for us or that we would prefer for ourselves. Talents and abilities are not evenly distributed among us. The circumstances that people come from are not the same. Fortune and misfortune do not, like falling snow, land on us evenly. The distribution of rewards people receive in the workplace is rarely equitable. The world of work, just like the world in general, has yet to evolve into a paradise where everyone enjoys plenty and where rewards are won through merit alone. We all know that hard work isn't always appreciated. Poor performers sometimes move ahead of their more reliable and competent counterparts. Jealousy, resentment, and competitiveness make relationships difficult and nice people don't always succeed. No, life isn't fair. It isn't fair in terms of our health or our endowments or our luck in being at the right place at the right time.

In our minds, success involves the character of the actions one takes, not in the tangible results they produce. After he left the presidency, John Quincy Adams returned to Congress and there, despite the gag rule against it, he spoke out against slavery. When asked why he persisted in what appeared to be a hopeless cause, Adams said, "Duty is ours, results are God's." This quotation captures the essence of what we mean by success. The fly fisherman does not measure his success in terms of the fishes he catches so much as he does in the way he fishes—how well he reads a stream, ties knots, selects the right flies, casts, presents the floating fly, lands his catch. Catching fish is thrilling but it isn't all there is to fishing. The furniture maker does not enjoy the praises others give for the beauty and quality of his pieces nearly as much as the pleasure he derives from the enjoyment of knowing how to design tables, chairs, and bureaus. Having a finished product to enjoy does not compare to the enjoyment he derives from selecting the right woods to use, and then shaping, carving, and finishing them. The way to the kind of success we are talking about requires using one's God-given capacities to their fullest possible extent.

DEVELOP WHAT IT TAKES TO MAKE THINGS HAPPEN

Assume Responsibility, Initiate Action, Accept the Consequences

"It is our duty as human beings to proceed as though the limits of our capabilities do not exist."

Teilhard de Chardin

On a late September morning many years ago a maintenance foreman named Arnold Effington came face to face with a problem common to practically every workplace around the world. Arnold was responsible for maintaining and repairing malfunctioning machinery at Anaconda's copper mine just south of Tucson, Arizona. Earlier that morning he sent a crew of men out to replace a broken piston on a hopper. Now, he wanted to check on their progress. As he drove up to the idle hopper, Arnold noticed that his crew was sitting down, talking among themselves. Turning off his pickup's engine, he saw one of the men jump up and begin inspecting the broken part. The others there stopped talking but remained seated. It was obvious to Arnold that his crew had been wasting time, doing nothing productive. He got mad but didn't want to let his anger show. So he simply asked, "What's going on?"

The men looked at each other briefly but no one spoke. Arnold pressed them again, this time with another question: "Why aren't you doing what I sent you here to do?"

One of the crew spoke, "We were waiting for you to tell us what to do." Arnold looked at the man but said nothing.

Another man spoke up, "We don't have the right parts. What do you want us to do? Besides, we need a larger wrench."

"You," said Arnold, pointing to one of the men, "Go to the supply room and get what you need." A pickup truck was parked nearby. These men did have a way of getting to the supply room to obtain the tools and parts they needed on their own, but they didn't make use of it. Instead, they sat around and talked, waiting for the foreman to come by and tell them what to do.

Arnold looked at the other men who remained seated and said, "The rest of you, start cleaning these rocks out of the way." Arnold waited until the man who went for the wrench returned with it. Then, as his crew began tearing apart the broken machinery, Arnold got into his truck and drove off.

It was plainly evident that not one of the work crew Arnold sent out to tackle a simple repair job was taking the initiative needed to move the job ahead. They were passive. What's worse, they didn't care. It wasn't their ore hopper that had a broken piston. It was the Anaconda Copper Company's problem, not theirs. What did they care if the piston got fixed that morning or that afternoon?

Shoulder the Responsibility to Get Things Done

Every day, whether you realize it or not, you face a fundamental choice. Will you accept responsibility for yourself and your actions or will you not accept responsibility? Will you take the initiative and get busy with what needs to be done at work, or will you not get busy and then create excuses for doing little? A sterling illustration of the importance of accepting responsibility came to public attention over a hundred years ago when Elbert Hubbard wrote his famous essay, "A Message to Garcia." Just before the beginning of the last century the United States faced a war with Spain over Cuba. President William McKinley needed vital information if U.S. soldiers were to cooperate with the insurgents and take control of the tiny island nation. McKinley wanted to know the number of Spanish troops and where they were, their combat skills and morale, the conditions of Cuba's roads, how well armed each side was, and what the Cubans needed. While American forces were being mobilized, the president needed someone to carry a message to and get vital information from the leader of the Cuban insurgents, a man named Garcia. "Where," asked the president, "can I find a man who will carry a message to Garcia?"

Colonel Arthur Wagner, head of the Bureau of Military Intelligence, had an immediate answer. He knew just the man for this delicate and dangerous mission. Without hesitation, Colonel Wagner told the president, "There is a young officer here in Washington; a lieutenant named Rowan, who will carry it for you."

"Send him," McKinley replied.

An hour later, at noon, Wagner met Rowan at the Army and Navy Club for lunch. While they ate, Colonel Wagner asked Lieutenant Rowan if he knew when the next boat to Jamaica would leave. Rowan didn't but he went immediately to find out. He returned shortly with the answer: the *Adirondack*, a British boat, would sail from New York the next day at noon. "Can you take that boat?" asked Wagner. Rowan said he could. "Then," said Wagner, "get ready to take it! Young man," Colonel Wagner continued, "you have been selected by the president to carry a message to General Garcia, who will be found somewhere in the eastern part of Cuba."

Garcia was somewhere in the mountain vastness of Cuba. No one knew exactly where. There were no telephones, no telegraph lines, no railroad lines, no paved roads. Someone was needed to get a message to him. It would be difficult and treacherous. There were seas to cross, night landings to make, jungles and mountains to traverse by foot and horseback, and enemies to avoid, lest the messenger be captured and the vital mission foiled. Rowan took the president's message and left. He would carry it to Garcia. Rowan didn't ask his superiors how he was to accomplish his mission. He didn't demand to know exactly where Garcia was or how to get to him. He didn't waste time demanding explanations as to how he was to slip past Spanish soldiers. These matters he would have to figure out for himself. He knew one thing and it was the most important thing for him: He would get President McKinley's message to Garcia.

Give someone a task to do and you will be able to tell immediately whether she can be depended on to get the job done by how she takes the order. Does the person ask for clarification on the nature of your expectations, the major details as to what the end product is that you have in mind so that she gets that same result clearly implanted in her mind? Or does he ask for details on how to proceed with things that he should be able to figure out for himself? Does the person ask, "Where do I find information on that?" or "What are the precise steps I must follow?" or "Why ask me to do it when Fred hasn't done a thing around here for days?" or "Don't you think I already have enough to do as it is?" These are not the questions that a man like Rowan would trifle with. He had his orders and he immediately busied himself to carry them out. He was the kind of man who would succeed in carrying the president's message to Garcia—and return to write about it.

A good way to succeed in the workplace is to develop the capacity to be responsible for yourself—to accept assignments and perform them on your own willingly and enthusiastically. Unlike weaker-willed individuals who wait to be told exactly what to do and how to do it, top performers take their ideas and put them into practice. When they see a job that needs doing, they go ahead and perform it. The difference between top performers in the workplace and those who accomplish little lies in the fact that achievers choose to assume responsibility. Each of us has what's known as free will. It is the power to be our own person—to make up our own mind, to choose to act as our mind and heart direct us, to accept assignments and figure out how to perform them on our own. Those who develop this capacity are the people we know as being dependable self-starters. Another benefit that comes to those who learn to accept responsibility is that they mature emotionally. Self-responsibility is the natural expression of adulthood. The more a person exercises the capacity to assume responsibility and initiate actions, the more he or she grows toward greater levels of autonomy. The healthy person looks upon her accomplishments as signs of growth. Having accomplished simple things, she eyes more difficult challenges worthy of her talents. Success builds on success.

Another useful outcome of assuming responsibility and taking initiative is that it teaches us the many valuable lessons that come from experience. From our experiences we learn that certain kinds of actions produce favorable consequences, while other kinds of actions lead to undesirable consequences. These are lessons that oftentimes cannot be taught in a classroom; they must be learned on one's own, through actually doing things. The more a person learns these many lessons the more that person becomes willing to take risks. As people learn to take on more responsibility they grow more confident in taking the initiative. These men and women we know as self-starters who can be depended upon to get things done without close supervision.

Care About What Happens

If you have spent any amount of time where people work, then surely you've noticed a few able-bodied men and women doing very little, perhaps next to nothing. We see them standing still, acting helpless, waiting to be told to "get busy." When confronted about their inaction, they are long on excuses and short on actions. Getting started—that's their problem. What is it that blocks their initiative? How can one develop the power to get started on one's own? To address these questions we need to look deeply into the inner tendencies of human nature that sometimes grow, like a strangling vine, in ways that hold people back.

One of the most debilitating inner tendencies to be found in humans is utter disregard for what happens. This feeling is aptly captured by the familiar line "It's not my concern." Late in the sixth century, Pope (later Saint) Gregory the Great is said to have compiled what we know today as the seven deadly sins—sins because they corrupt judgment as to what is good and evil, cloud the conscience, and remove the hesitancy to say no to self-destructive tendencies. Three of the seven are "hot" sins—anger, lust, and gluttony. These are aggressive and loaded with passion. Three other sins are called "cold" sins—avarice, pride, and envy—sins filled with hatred and calculating thoughts and actions. Sloth is different. It is neither hot nor cold, neither heated aggressiveness nor coldhearted calculation. It is idleness, passivity, laziness.

Slothfulness is far worse than mere laziness or idleness. It is rooted in an "I don't care" feeling. A person might be lazy for all sorts of reasons and shaken out of it by various means. But a person who does not care is harder to reach, harder to set into motion because no desire exists to excite into action. Sloth is not the same as stupidity. A slothful person can see what should be done in a situation. Ignorance and dullness of mind are not what holds the slothful person back from purposeful action. The slothful person simply does not care enough about things to assume responsibility for what happens or to take the initiative to do anything. Sadly, sloth causes people to waste whatever talents they may possess. Over time these talents tend to wither away.

On a plot of land at the eastern edge of Oxford, Ohio, people in our town used to plant and tend vegetable gardens. It was a community activity that brought a spirit of hope and excitement and neighborliness to Oxford every spring. Markers divided the many garden plots, which individuals or entire families tended. It's a law of life that only hard work produces fruitful results. With vegetable gardens especially, the relationship between effort and results is direct. And the work must proceed in a certain sequence. First comes tilling the soil, preparing it for planting. Next, seeds are sown—beets, corn, green beans, carrots, turnips, cauliflower, whatever the plot tender wants and hopes to harvest—these must be planted carefully. After that, plants need regular amounts of water. A nearby stream ran just west of Oxford's garden plots from which water could be hauled to keep the seedlings moist. Day after day one could see people cheerfully carrying containers of the much-needed source of life to their thirsty plants. As the spring rains gave way to intense July dry spells and blistering temperatures, the clay soil dried and hardened. Weeds sprang up. Summer vegetables, as folks soon realized, were not something one got for free. More work was necessary, hard work of weeding, watering, tilling, and keeping pesky insects from eating the growing plants.

From the highway nearby anyone driving past the garden plots could see people there tending their crops. From that distance it looked like abundance was everywhere. But up close things were different. After just a few weeks it became clear which plots were being cared for with more love and attention than others. Some plots were immaculately groomed. The produce growing on them thrived. Other plots, which may have had good beginnings, appeared to be headed for sad endings, with their plants shriveling up from lack of moisture and weeds crowding out their chances for survival. Could it be that the owners of these plots stopped caring? It appeared so. Sloth does this same sort of thing to our lives. It allows possibilities to die, hopes to be crowded out by weeds, insects to eat away and kill off good life. When a person stops caring, passivity sets in and idleness prevails. Work goes undone. The possibilities for good that might have grown wither and die.

Rise Above Passivity

The first story of recorded history—the story of Adam and Eve in the Garden of Eden—can be interpreted as a human failing from passivity. As we know, the serpent tempted Eve, as Adam stood by passively. Adam could have guarded the garden as God told him to do and fought the serpent. He didn't. He could have called to God for help—"What should I do?" Adam didn't do that either. Instead, he remained passive. He had a chance to take responsibility, to show initiative, to act purposefully, but he didn't. Maybe he was lazy. He certainly didn't think of himself as being responsible for providing his own food and shelter. These were given to him. In a sense, Adam was asleep to the idea of work and responsibility. Now when Eve ate from the tree of knowledge of good and evil and got Adam to do the same, things changed. They awoke to responsibility, to the necessity of work, challenges that men and women have lived with ever after.

Initiative is the vital element that causes people to solve problems while they are small and before they grow large and out of control. It is what spells the difference between ordinary and exceptional customer service. And it is the underlying reason why some people continually make improvements at work while others do not. Responsibility acceptance is what makes things begin to happen that would not otherwise happen. Without a feeling of responsibility for one's self, for what one thinks, and for what one does, a person cannot be counted on to take the initiative and to follow through with consistent actions.

A young woman we know named Tracy told us about an experience that she had while working as a lifeguard at a private swim club. During a party at this swim club, Tracy got a whiff of something, and she didn't like it. She discovered a strong odor of chlorine coming from a back room. Tracy investigated further and found that the pool's pump had sprung a leak. Chlorine was not being pumped into the pool. To her, this looked like a serious problem. She had heard about the dangers of chlorine gas and she worried about the possibilities of untreated water in a public pool. These thoughts convinced her to act on her own instincts. So, without wasting time, she made everyone get out of the pool and then she phoned the local fire department. After the fire department personnel arrived and inspected the situation, they told Tracy that she did the right thing. There was a danger. And they told her and the swim club's manager that the pool should not reopen until the leaky pump was fixed or replaced.

The other day I (Tom Idinopulos) stopped at a home and garden store near my residence to purchase a pair of scissors. Upon entering the store, I approached a clerk who was standing behind a cash register and inquired where I might find what I wanted. "We don't sell scissors," he told me. I thought it odd that a large store that appeared to carry every possible household item that people might need would not stock a simple pair of scissors. So, I walked through the store, optimistically looking for what I wanted. Seeing another clerk who was stocking shelves, I asked her about scissors. "Oh yes," she said. "Let me show you." This clerk took me to a large wall display that had a rack of scissors. Initiative—that's what this clerk had, and her initiative made her a valuable employee. It is sad to think of the number of working men and women who lack initiative. And because they do not have it, they are ineffective, worth very little to their employer—and they are probably miserable in their jobs too because they don't experience the fun of finding things to do and then doing them on their own.

Be Responsible for Yourself

If you'd like a surefire formula for failure, here's one that works every time: Be passive, indecisive, unwilling to act. Run away from your responsibilities. Sit back instead of stepping up to your obligations. Be preoccupied with the trivial. Blame others or your circumstances when things don't work out. These are all excellent ways to play the part of the escapist and accomplish little.

The world is filled with two sorts: those who do things and those who are quick to offer excuses for why they didn't get anything done. We naturally admire those men and women whose actions make a difference, those we know we can depend on to accept responsibility and initiate action. These are the people who are known for their steady follow-through efforts, the ones who perform the "heavy lifting."

Taking responsibility for yourself involves taking yourself seriously. It is a cornerstone to good mental health and an indispensable element in making things happen. We see this quality in those who get things done. Here's an illustration of what we mean. Suppose you realized that technology had passed you by, that your computer skills needed a boost? A healthy person faces reality honestly and takes action. This is exactly what the head of the Aircraft Engine Division of a major U.S. corporation once did. He realized that he didn't know what he believed a person in his position should know about computers and what their information access and processing capabilities are. So, instead of denying his shortcoming he accepted its existence and decided to do something positive to correct it. He asked a top technical person to tutor him in the information-sharing possibilities of computers for two hours every other week—the tutoring went on for nearly two years. This executive knew that running a high-tech business required being on top of this aspect of computer technology. He did something to make that happen. For those who want to boost their ability to accept responsibility, here are twelve suggestions—think of them as ideals you can check yourself against every day. Say to yourself, I am responsible for:

1. Achieving my goals and desires.
2. My choices and actions—dealing with stress effectively, weathering disappointments.
3. My behavior, especially with other people.
4. How I use my time, what I choose to do ahead of other things.
5. What I worry over and spend time thinking about.
6. How well I communicate with others.
7. The way I treat my body and take care of my health, physical and emotional.
8. My spiritual development.
9. The people I associate with and the friends I keep.
10. My personal happiness, whether I am positive or negative.
11. Choosing and accepting the values I live by
12. How I feel about myself.

Turn Your Ideas into Actions

It does not require great intellect to recognize the difference between the doers of our world and those who are quick to offer up excuses for why they were unable to begin even the simplest of tasks. One of the best ways to get noticed and move your career along in a positive direction is to turn your ideas into concrete actions. The next time you see something that should be done, ask yourself, "What am I going to do about it?" I (Charles Watson) recall an incident about a man who worked in the personnel department at the corporate headquarters of a *Fortune* 500 firm. This man offered more than just a suggestion that was badly needed at the time and top management liked it because of how it was presented. The story begins when the company this man (we'll call him Carl to protect his anonymity) worked for decided to sell one of its operating divisions, a forest products company. After officers of his firm examined the offers received they selected one. The acquiring company was willing to buy the entire division, although they were really interested in only the acreage of forestland that the division owned. The acquiring company wasn't going to keep the mill operation going.

Carl thought about all the employees working in the division's mill who would probably lose their jobs. What about them? Who was going to help them relocate to other jobs? He thought that his company—the one that was selling its division—should do something to assist all these loyal employees who were about to be out of work through no fault of their own. So, Carl sat down and drew up a plan, titling it "How to Handle Mass Separations: Helping Good Employees Find Work." His proposal had a stated purpose, a step-by-step action plan and a cost figure. Up it went through the chain of command. In a short while, the company's vice chairman of the board called Carl to his office. What the vice chairman liked was the fact that Carl presented not just a simple suggestion, but a complete plan. The vice chairman told Carl, "I want you to be at the mill Monday morning and begin implementing your plan." All too often, people have ideas about what should be done but little in the way of specifics as to how to implement their proposals. Management likes initiative when it has more to it than just a suggestion. They want implementation methods too.

The Importance of Believing in Your Abilities

Henry Ford, the man whose name represents the automobile to millions of people around the globe, is reported to have said, "Whether you think you can or you can't, you're usually right." Wouldn't you like to have the power of self-confidence that's needed to tackle the difficult and succeed at it? Of course, we'd all nod in agreement with the idea that if anything is going to happen it is up to someone to make it happen. The "glitch" is whether a person believes she or he is capable of causing it to come about. In the back of everyone's mind there lingers the question, "Am I smart enough, capable enough, powerful enough, and motivated enough to make it happen?" The fact is people will not act on things when they think their abilities are too puny to handle the difficulties found in tough assignments.

When confronting any difficult endeavor, each of us will ask ourselves, "Can I do it?" Professor Albert Bandura of Stanford University has spent a lifetime studying this important idea, which he calls *self-efficacy*. Simply stated, self-efficacy means a person's beliefs about his or her abilities to produce specific results that require one's actions and effort. According to Professor Bandura, people with strong self-efficacy will generally accomplish difficult assignments and feel good about themselves. These people feel sure of their capabilities and they accept one challenge after another. They see difficult tasks as exciting challenges to be mastered, not as threats to be avoided. A person with a strong sense of self-efficacy finds enjoyment in doing the difficult because it stretches his abilities. People with high self-efficacy will stick with a difficult task until it is completed as a matter of self-respect, even when the chances of failure appear high.

In contrast to those people who accomplish much and enjoy doing so are those who spend their time complaining instead of achieving. These people are their own worst enemy because they have a weak sense of self-efficacy. They doubt their capabilities. If something looks difficult they fear it. Seeing challenges as personal threats to be avoided, those with a weak sense of self-efficacy choose only the simplest and easiest of tasks. And their commitment to completing these soft jobs is so weak that they give up whenever the slightest obstacle arises. It's easy to spot a person with low self-efficacy. They dwell on their inadequacies. They worry and complain about their weaknesses. And they whine about their past failures, which are numerous. The sad truth is that these people are constantly saying to themselves, "You are a loser; you'll never succeed at anything."

The best way for anyone to regain a sense of self-assurance is by accomplishing something meaningful. Accomplishments build competency. Competency builds confidence. And more confidence leads to greater accomplishments. Telling people that they are capable may help get them started, but without success authentic confidence—a strong sense of self-efficacy—is impossible. The classic children's story of the *Little Engine that Could*, familiar to many, captures the essential element of what we are talking about here. Its "I think I can" is followed by effort that succeeds. As the little engine builds up steam and moves the train ahead it changes from "I think I can" to "I know I can."

How many leaders do you know who complain about their employees? "What's wrong with people these days?" they ask. "Why can't they perform better? Why do they need constant supervision?" These leaders complain about how difficult it is for them to elicit high-level performances from subordinates who appear not to care. Yet if we ask each of these leaders, "Is there anything you are doing about it?" Invariably their answer is, "No." The leader who complains and tries nothing to change the situation is, in fact, a person who is not accepting responsibility. Without the acceptance of responsibility, a person will show no initiative and take no purposeful actions to change matters. If you examine your complaints you will come face to face with a challenge. It is this: Will you turn your complaints into actions? Ask yourself, "What will I do about this situation to make it the way I'd prefer it to be?"

We once knew a remarkable man who did this very thing—he turned his complaints into purposeful actions. Shortly after he was made manager of a steel plant many years ago, a man named Fred decided he'd change things, not whine and complain about them. The problem Fred faced was that his plant's employees were passive. Their morale was terrible. They took no pride in themselves or their work. This was largely because the previous plant manager insisted on making every decision. The old manager so controlled everything that went on, large and small, that employees grew passive. They had given up on the idea of ever being in charge of anything that went on where they worked. They felt they were mere cogs in a gigantic machine and had no say in what happened. Everything flowed from the boss. All decisions required his approval, his final OK. At first, Fred complained about the situation—the laziness, the low morale, the "Who cares?" attitude. One day, an idea entered Fred's mind. What good was all his complaining doing? At that moment Fred realized that something needed to be changed. And that something had to begin with himself. Fred realized that he could not make all the decisions himself. He knew he had to get employees to assume more responsibility and show initiative.

Here's how Fred handled the situation that confronted him. Whenever an employee came to him with a problem in need of a solution, Fred would ask that person what he thought. "How would you solve the problem?" he'd ask. Sometimes the employee had a pretty good idea, which Fred would discuss with the person further. By treating employees in this way, Fred slowly and subtly began to convince them that they had good minds and that they were able to think and act for themselves. Change occurred slowly. After a year's time, productivity at the plant began to pick up. And it kept rising. Two years later, higher-ups in his company considered Fred's the best-run plant in the company. Bottlenecks that, earlier, had been created by having to wait for the top man to decide were gone. Pride increased. Sloppy work caused by the previous "I don't care" attitude disappeared. Employees saw what needed doing and they took the initiative to do it without fear that their bosses might disapprove.

When Duty Calls, Say Yes!

If you don't accept responsibility for completing work on time, you're headed for trouble. We heard recently about a young woman who had this difficulty. Dana graduated from college a couple of years before this incident took place and she had moved up in her company because of her intelligence and pleasing personality. Being a social person, Dana was well suited for her job in customer service. She was on a team that had responsibility for finding ways her company could better serve its customers. The boss asked Dana's team to identify those things the company was failing to do well in terms of customer service and to recommend solutions. This project required her team to survey customers by telephone and hold focus group interviews. Once the data were collected, the team faced the task of making sense out of what they had heard and learned. This phase of the project required lengthy meetings, which frequently stretched into weekday evenings and sometimes into the weekends.

Dana's team needed more time to finish its assignment before a scheduled Monday morning presentation, but only a few more days remained and these were Friday, Saturday, and Sunday. Dana wanted to get away for the weekend with her friends and have fun. She was dead tired from work and felt she deserved some fun. These wants caused her to decide to go ahead with her social plans and then try to think of a reasonable-sounding excuse on Monday morning for her absence. But as the hours ticked by on Friday afternoon and quitting time neared, Dana had misgivings. She decided that her fun would have to come second to her duties at work. She could always go skiing another time. Whereas getting a good job would be more difficult—and costly.

How would you respond the next time you are faced with a call to duty when another option is more inviting? One important difference between people who are least employable—people who cannot seem to hold a job—and those people who do hold down steady jobs and move ahead is the willpower to stick with the difficult and unpleasant. Imagine this scene. It's a Sunday afternoon and men are gathered watching a late afternoon football game. They are having a good time but one of them wants to move the "fun" up a notch. He breaks out some drugs and offers them to the others. The person with a very short time perspective, who is incapable of saying "no" to what might be immediately gratifying—not to say illegal—is unable to resist. What this person most needs to help straighten out his life is the willingness to accept responsibility, to rise above being a victim of his own immediate desires.

Accept the Consequences of Your Actions

An important quality that many people never master is precisely this, the willingness to accept responsibility when things go wrong. The person who admits to mistakes when they occur and faces head-on a stiff chewing-out from the boss is a rarity. Why do so many people have this difficulty? We know of people in our organization, and you probably know of some in your organization too, who are driven by one thing—to get the approval of others. So needy are these folks for the approval of others, that they demand compliments and attention. They are self-absorbed, too dependent on having others say good things about them. Praise is fine when it is deserved but praise can also work on people in a negative way. Look deeper and you'll see that these people are their own worst enemy, because above all else they fear criticism. They will do practically anything to avoid it. They take on just those assignments that they feel secure in, knowing these will bring them praise. And they will refuse to take steps on their own whenever they are unsure about how those higher up in their organization will react. If all a person hears is praise, deserved and undeserved, that person starts believing he or she is not just flawless but also above criticism.

Of course, we all fear failure. That's natural. What we need to recognize is that fear of failure can be both a good thing and a bad thing. On the one hand it can keep a person from doing really dumb things, risky things that may harm others or property. But on the other hand we need to see how the driving need to escape blame frequently leads people into becoming their own worst enemy. This is because in trying to avoid blame they have no other way out but to lie. And lies are always found out either sooner or later and when they are discovered, the liar's reputation is ruined or seriously damaged. We have a friend named Frank who owns and operates a business that manufactures and installs imitation marble sinks, tubs, and shower enclosures. Frank installs these products himself. He depends on his men to load his truck with the right products and necessary materials the evening before the next day's installations. One day Frank arrived on an important job only to discover that Tom and John had left out the sinks he needed. Later that day, when Frank returned to the plant, he asked Tom about it. Tom said, "I didn't load the truck. John did." Frank then went to John and asked him about the mistake. "No," said John. "I didn't load the truck. It was Stan." Stan had quit the previous day, so there wasn't anyone on hand for Frank to blame. But Frank is not a stupid man. He knew that either Tom or John was lying to him and his respect for each of them dropped a little bit because of how they tried to escape blame.

How you handle your mistakes can either make you or break you. Everything depends on your willingness to accept the consequences of your actions. When he was Chairman and CEO of Westinghouse in Pittsburgh, Pennsylvania, Douglas Danforth told us, "When I make a mistake, I tell them (the board of directors). They love it. And they are more supportive of me than if I tried to hide it." The next time you make a mistake, take the initiative to admit it right away and then go ahead and do something positive to correct it. People will admire you for your honesty and your initiative. You will feel better about yourself too—you really will. There is a man in our town named Austin who owns a small business. Austin's Floor Store sells and installs carpet, linoleum, and other kinds of floor coverings. Once, after installing a carpet for an elderly woman, she phoned Austin. There was something in the carpet, she believed, that was giving her headaches. What could Austin do? Without hesitation, Austin sent out a crew to remove the new carpet and reinstall her old carpet. Austin told the woman, the new carpet wasn't acceptable to you, so there will be no charge. That happened over ten years ago when Austin had only two trucks traveling around town, delivering carpets, and his employees installing them. Today, Austin's Floor Store has many more delivery trucks on the road. His new store is larger and more inviting than his previous location was. He employs more people now too. His business thrives.

Taking responsibility for one's actions is a vital element of self-esteem. It is something that cannot be built on false praise. There is really only one way to earn well-deserved praise: do something that's praiseworthy. In shops and factories all across the land able and well-meaning men and women are hard at work turning out products that you and I will use. How carefully they inspect their plants' output is one reliable indicator of how well they accept their responsibility to place workable products into their customers' hands. We learned about a man named Jim Rooney who was a vice president of manufacturing for Zenith—and he took his responsibilities seriously. Once Rooney shut down production of color televisions in Zenith's St. Louis plant because some of the parts they were using were defective and the sets weren't meeting quality standards. Rooney told John Nevin, Zenith's CEO at the time, "I don't get upset when a part of the manufacturing process gets out of control and you've got to shut down the plant in order to maintain your standards. That's unavoidable in American business. I do get upset when I find someone who will take his mistakes, pack them up in a box, and ship them to our customers."

Common Ways People Fail in Accepting Responsibility

The ways in which we can fail to accept responsibility for ourselves are many. Let's review some of the more common ones here.

Blaming Others When Things Go Wrong. A supervisor is given responsibility for an important assignment that requires the efforts of several individual contributors. One of the contributors fails to do his part or does it poorly. Rather than get someone else to help or to redo the weak part of the work, the supervisor blames the slacker but doesn't fix the defect.

Blaming One's Circumstances. In an emotion-filled meeting one person makes unkind and hurtful remarks to another person. Rather than admitting to being uncivil and apologizing, the intemperate speaker blames the tense meeting for her angry outburst, saying, "I just cannot control my temper. You made me so angry that I could not help myself."

Waiting for Explicit Direction. An employee waits passively until his boss comes by to explain exactly how to perform the assigned work. Instead of going to the boss and asking for more information or help or even trying to perform the work in the best way he knows how, he waits passively for directions.

Being Too Needy. Dominated by the desire for recognition, an employee fishes for praise and compliments from others rather than concentrating on just doing his work.

Fearing Criticism Above All Else. A person refuses to state his position, fearful it might not align with the beliefs of those in power or the opinion of an authority figure who is present.

Ignoring One's Health and Well-Being. A business owner refuses to take time off to get away and relax. She is focused on making her firm succeed but untrusting of those under her. She fears her employees might not handle things at work as well as she might herself. In the back of her mind she knows that she is harming her health and her family relationships. Still, she keeps up her relentless work pace. When her doctor suggests she slow down, she has a ready excuse, "I'm needed at work." Even when she does get sick, she refuses to accept the fact that her behavior is the cause. Instead she tells herself, "My body got sick and it made me take time off to rest."

Playing the Part of the Victim. A worker develops the habit of feeling sorry for himself. Whatever difficulty or unpleasantness visits the workplace, this person sees himself as the victim of its ill effects. When something gets between him and his own comfort and well-being, he whines and complains.

Remaining Passive. Two people have a conflict, each waits passively for the other to do something. Each avoids taking responsibility for achieving a resolution and restoring a damaged relationship.

MAKE THE MOST OF WHO YOU ARE

Understand Yourself, Accept Yourself, Be Yourself

"We are always stronger when we do not try to fight reality."

Nathaniel Branden

In a story appearing in *Entrepreneur* magazine a few years ago, Barry Farber told of a sales rep who once worked for him. This rep wasn't doing very well. "At first," said Farber, "I couldn't understand why. He had a great personality; people thought he was a natural-born salesperson. But he wasn't making sales. So I went along with him on some sales calls to find out what the problem was."

It didn't take Farber long to realize what was happening. As soon as this rep came face to face with a customer, his personality changed. His true self seemed to disappear, and another self took over. His speech pattern and tone changed. He suddenly became a different person, as he took the customer through a robotic, by-the-book sales presentation straight out of Selling 101. As he stepped into his salesperson mode, he stepped right out of the sale. Barry Farber's advice to the rep was direct and simple: Just be yourself.

Learn How to Be *For* Yourself

It cannot be emphasized too strongly that making the most of who you are begins with knowing how to *just be yourself*. But what does this actually mean? And, how does one do that? For starters it means understanding and accepting yourself. This is not something we do naturally. It is something we must learn and work at doing every day. To be yourself you also need to value yourself, respect yourself, and stand up for your right to be yourself. You can make the most of who you are by being "for yourself." This is your birthright as a human being.

Our capacity for self-assessment is one of the most helpful human qualities we can exercise. It is the basis for how we control our actions and choose to live up to high standards. It is astonishing to see what can happen whenever a person compares his actual self with the idealized person whom he would prefer to be. An excellent way to improve both yourself and the quality of your work is to compare your actions with what you think the best way of acting is. We once had at a local bank a teller who was known for his tendency to treat people abruptly. We called him Grouchy George. While he was accurate and speedy in serving customers, he was also unwilling to smile and make people feel welcome. Then something dramatic happened. Although we were never sure whether it was a year-end performance appraisal or something someone said to Grouchy George, we do know that he changed. Somehow George glimpsed something about himself that he didn't like. It caused him to begin smiling at his customers and greeting them with a friendly word. It is sad to realize that all those many years while George was grouchy on the outside he was quite a different person on the inside. Surely he must have seen that too. Some folks said he was just shy and unsure of himself. Maybe he was. What we do know is that George started smiling at his customers and they started smiling back at him. Smiles and friendly greetings made customers feel more welcome. They began to enjoy their experience at the bank more. And George began enjoying his work more too.

You can never tell beforehand what might cause you to look at yourself. When he headed the McDonnell-Douglas Aircraft Corporation, Sanford McDonnell told me (Charles) about an experience he had that illustrates this very phenomenon. He told me that as a Boy Scout leader he had always been impressed with the impact the Scout Oath and Laws had on boys. One day, after talking to scouts about the oath and laws, McDonnell said that he asked himself, "What am I doing to live up to them?" He said that upon self-examination, he saw areas in his own life where he was falling short. Then he got to thinking, *Do we have a code of ethics at McDonnell Douglas?* They didn't. So he assembled a small task force of top people and told them,

"Here is the Boy Scouts of America Oath and Laws. I want you to create a code of conduct for everyone in our organization that looks like that. I want you to cover every point in there."

Awakening to one's faults does not always produce agreeable outcomes. With some people it can be quite upsetting; and these negative emotions can sometimes turn into bigger problems for them than we might imagine. Opening a person's eyes to a personal deficiency can burden that person with so much shame and feelings of inferiority that they give up on themselves. The gulf between what they see in themselves and what they would like to see might appear to be so great that they perceive their failures as insurmountable, even unforgivable. When this happens they will worry themselves sick with feelings of dissatisfaction. The sad reality is that these people cannot accept themselves as persons. They give up on themselves. If they are overwhelmed by feelings of shame, guilt, or inferiority, humans can turn to rebellious patterns, lapse into states of self-pity that are all-consuming, or they can become frozen by apathy and inertia. Sometimes they stop being on their own side. If they are deeply dissatisfied with who they are, they may masquerade as persons they are not—the shy person becomes aggressive, the timid woman speaks effusively, the fearful man acts with bluster, and the insecure individual plays the part of a big shot.

Being "for yourself" involves refusing to give up on yourself in spite of whatever mess you may have made of yourself. It means standing up for yourself. It means seeing your possibilities as well as your shortcomings. It means knowing your limits and knowing your potentialities. It means knowing how to escape the traps of false humility and false pride. False humility exists when a person refuses to acknowledge her strengths, the lovely aspects of her character and disposition, her talents—the talents she has developed and applied and those she has yet to discover and put to use. False pride is present when a person puffs himself up. And like proud peacocks parading about with their feathers spread out, he brags about his achievements and talents and pretends to be larger than he really is.

In collecting anecdotes and examples of how people harm themselves in the workplace, people we listened to described numerous examples of annoying coworkers. These annoying people were their own worst enemy because they created personae from their imaginations of idealized selves that were inconsistent with the real persons underneath. Others said that these people had a way of trying to feed their egos by self-delusional and self-created images and then believing their imaginings were real. But their puffery didn't fool anyone other than themselves. Coworkers saw through these layers of imagination and lost respect for them as persons. They had little patience for their puffery and didn't accept them as authentic, which they were not.

Get to Know Yourself

A fifty-six-year-old mechanical engineer named Matt stopped what he was doing long enough to tell us his story. In explaining his typical workday, Matt revealed a pattern of tendencies and actions he could not seem to shake free of that kept him from understanding himself. Here is what Matt said:

> From 7:00 A.M., when I leave the house, until I crash back into bed, my days are filled with solving problems and meeting my obligations. I wonder what would get done if I weren't there to do it. Yet, as much as I complain about how busy my life is, secretly I think I like it. It makes me feel important. I accepted six special assignments and agreed to serve on three committees last year. Why? Because I thought they'd fail without my expertise. Yes, I'm a busy person. But, you know what? I think I keep myself busy to avoid something.
>
> I have asked myself why I try to stay so busy. Part of the reason, I suppose, is that I'm a responsible person. And, I think I have something to contribute. But that's not the entire story. I sometimes feel that there's a bigger reason. I suspect there is something about having myself on my hands with nothing to do that frightens me. This feeling bothers me so much that I make a point of staying busy, always having something left on my plate to do. To be perfectly honest, I do all sorts of things to avoid myself. I don't think I'm unusual. Still, I wonder who I am. Maybe I have hidden talents yet to be discovered and put to use. Something inside me makes me wonder if I am the person I could become.
>
> I wonder what would happen if, instead of seeking diversions and filling my days with activities, I spent time thinking. I've never thought about important things, things like: Who am I? What am I doing with my life? Am I happy? But these are too hard to deal with. It's easier to glide by, doing things. Besides, no one can ever answer these questions for sure.

This case is an illustration of how, by staying busy, a person can escape ever having to do something he secretly fears doing: facing himself. We told Matt about a friend of ours—she's a medical receptionist—who explained an effective approach that she uses for understanding herself. She said that she finds learning about her innermost self both thrilling and valuable. Here is what she does: every morning she awakens thirty minutes before her husband and children do. She brushes her teeth, gets a cup of coffee, and goes into a pantry where she reads. She cherishes these times. She allows herself private quiet time to think. The ancient wisdom from the Bible gives us this same good advice, "Be still and think." It is good advice to follow, because something wonderful happens inside us when we are alone and our minds are working.

Ordinary people report extraordinary outcomes from these times of quiet contemplation: creative ideas fill their minds, they feel intense joy, and they reach deeper insights about self, others, and difficult situations they are facing. One person we know told us what happened to him through devoting a few minutes each day to read from the novels of Charles Dickens. He told us that through his reading he experienced the fascinating characters in Dickens' novels. Their lives, their actions, and their thoughts and experiences, he finds, make him more acutely aware of himself—what he most loves, fears, wants, and hates, in himself and in others. During these quiet hours of reading and reflection, this man slowly, almost imperceptibly, came to understand and appreciate his innermost feelings—and he respects them.

It takes a certain kind of courage to face oneself in quiet reflection. It is easy to give in to familiar impulses: to hunt for distractions, to keep busy, to insist that something other than ourselves needs our attention. Just as an organization goes through planning sessions—call them times to think about the future and reflect inwardly—so too a person does well by doing the same kind of thing, reflecting. Being busy isn't necessarily a bad thing but being too busy to plan for the future is a prescription for disaster. The woman who avoids examining her inner life likewise invites disasters. There is the disaster of not knowing the person she can be; the disaster of not doing those things that she is best suited to do; and the disaster of not developing her talents—talents that, otherwise, might be put into useful service and lead to unimaginable satisfaction.

Respect Your Inner Voice

We live in a world composed of things visible and things invisible. One of the more familiar unseen realities is a tiny voice that resides within each one of us. As if coming from the innermost regions of our being, this voice speaks to us. It speaks not in words but in impulses, feelings of awe, uplifting joy. Many people think of it as our "inner voice." Our conscience is part of this inner voice but there is more to it than just that. Our inner voice connects us to our powers of reason, judgment, creativity, and emotion. One of the more important questions that your inner voice constantly poses to you is, "Are you doing what you ought to be doing?" In the context of work this question can have to do with things like your choice of career, your decision to tackle one assignment instead of another, your choice to take responsibility for something or not, or what you decide to do at a given moment in time. Why is this inner voice phenomenon important? Why ought we to pay it any attention?

Maybe you have realized the existence of your inner voice and its patient yet insistent calls to your heart, urging you to be the authentic person you were created to be. It may be helpful for you to hear the experiences of a young man we met recently. We won't use his real name here but simply refer to him as Jack instead. Jack started out on one career path he planned on following right out of college. Being smart and hardworking, Jack moved ahead in his organization. He experienced many of the same bumps and setbacks everyone else experiences, but overall he did quite well and moved up in his company. Now, despite the increased responsibilities he has and his many past advancements and pay increases, Jack feels unsettled. Something deep within troubles him. Reading between the lines of Jack's actual words, we sensed that Jack feels that regardless of how well he performs he does not experience contentment, a sense of lasting satisfaction. It is as if he is asking himself, "Is this all there really is to life and work?" As we see it, Jack's inner voice is at work, doing what it is intended to do, calling out to him, saying, "You are not doing what you are authentically suited to do. Try something else."

Quite likely you have heard of Kris Kristofferson, one of America's most gifted songwriters. He traveled in the company of other country music greats—Johnny Cash, Willie Nelson, and Waylon Jennings. We bring Kristofferson's story to your notice because it illustrates how a person already successful in one line of work nonetheless listened to something deep within himself and moved his life in a direction for which he proved to be even better suited. A bright and capable student, Kristofferson graduated Phi Beta Kappa from Pomona College, where he studied creative writing. He continued his studies on a Rhodes scholarship at Oxford University, where he earned a master's degree in English literature. He married and joined the Army. Like his father, he became a pilot. He learned to fly helicopters. While on assignment in West Germany in the 1960s Kristofferson organized soldiers' bands and wrote songs. People liked his songs and encouraged him to pursue his special gift. In 1965, the Army assigned Kristofferson to West Point, where he was to teach English. But something that happened in June of 1965 while he was in Nashville during a two-week leave caused him to change his career course. Kristofferson decided that he really wanted to become a country songwriter instead of a career military man. He resigned his commission barely two months before President Johnson pushed America further into the Vietnam conflict. We can only speculate what might have become of Kris Kristofferson had he not changed career direction. But what's important is that we do know that he did. And because he did we are enriched by his many hits such as "Me and Bobby McGee," "Help Me Make it Through the Night," and "For the Good Times."

The word "failure" generally brings up a host of unpleasant thoughts and feelings. We fear failure and we try to avoid it. Yet it comes into every life. Have you ever considered the possibility that something good might come from a failure? Sometimes your failures are really blessings in disguise. They might be signals that you are moving in a wrong direction. Consider the story that Steve Jobs, cofounder of Apple Computer, told in a 2005 commencement address at Stanford University. It dealt with failure and his response to it. Needing capital to expand in the beginning months of their fledgling personal computer business, Jobs and his partner Steve Wozniak incorporated, making them minor shareholders subject to the decisions of a board of directors. Jobs explained what happened: "As Apple grew we hired someone who I thought was very talented to run the company with me, and for the first year or so things went well. But then our visions of the future began to diverge and eventually we had a falling out. When we did, our Board of Directors sided with him. So, at thirty, I was out. And very publicly out. What had been the focus of my entire adult life was gone, and it was devastating. I really didn't know what to do for a few months. I felt that I had let the previous generation of entrepreneurs down—that I had dropped the baton as it was being passed to me.... I was a very public failure and I even thought about running away from the Valley. But something slowly began to dawn on me—I still loved what I did. The turn of events at Apple had not changed that one bit. I had been rejected, but I was still in love. And so I decided to start over."

And did he ever start over. Jobs started doing again what he did best, create creative companies. He started a company called NeXT, another one called Pixar and then, after that, he oversaw development of the iPod, and he continues developing new technologies and new enterprises to exploit them. Jobs advised the Stanford graduates he addressed that day in 2005, "Your work is going to fill a large part of your life, and the only way to be truly satisfied is to do what you believe is great work. And the only way to do great work is to love what you do. If you haven't found it yet, keep looking. Don't settle. As with all matters of the heart, you'll know when you find it."

Make the Most of Your Real Self, Not Your Desired Self

It is widely held that a mark of an admirable personality is to set high targets for oneself and then achieve them through sheer willpower, determination, and hard work. The roster of highly successful persons is filled with names of those who, with seemingly little natural ability, overcame their ordinariness to record spectacular accomplishments. Because he bet on baseball, the name Pete Rose may never enter Major League Baseball's Hall of Fame. But Rose will always be regarded as the finest example of how determination and consistent effort carried a ball player of ordinary abilities to become the all-time leader in base hits.

It would be deceptively easy to conclude that each of us ought to fix our sights on some admirable target and work until we reach that goal. But is this always realistic? Could we not be making ourselves into our own worst enemy by pursuing purposes to which we are ill-suited? Of course we could; and when we do we will find ourselves paying stiff penalties. This is why it is important to make a distinction between your ideal self and your real self. Your ideal self is the person you long to become. Your authentic self is the person you really are. Whenever a person tries to achieve in realms for which he or she is not fitted, we find gross maladjustment. Nothing, we may think, is finer than a young person about to blossom and become a productive adult, to have a goal, a purpose in mind for their life. "I want to become a dancer," a small girl tells her parents. "I intend to be mathematician and work for NASA," says another youngster. Yet it is possible that these children may not possess the right temperament or have the necessary talents to succeed in these fields. A weasel trying to be a black bear is an absurdity. Still, many people try to force themselves into roles and work for which they are equally ill-equipped.

A friend named Bill Haney, who once taught at Northwestern University and wrote a leading textbook in interpersonal communication, often told of an experience he had as he struggled to find the right niche for himself. At a young age Bill got it into his head that he was destined to be a chemist. On his eleventh birthday Bill got a chemistry set, and for hours on end he would mix different compounds and elements, causing various chemical reactions to take place in beakers and test tubes. In his daydreams he visualized himself, some day in the future, wearing a lab coat and working in a chemistry laboratory, creating wondrous scientific breakthroughs and thrilling the scientific community. But later on, when he got to college, Bill had a bigger and more difficult lesson to learn than chemistry principles. His abilities and the demands of mastering chemistry were ill-matched to each other. After serving in the Army, Bill entered college. There he enrolled in his first college-level chemistry course. Then came his first exam and the result was very disappointing—he scored a C−. His next exam grade was no better. What Bill had not counted on was that to be good in chemistry he needed to be pretty good in math—Bill was never very good in math. After more disappointments and more bad grades in chemistry courses, Bill realized that he was not cut out to be a chemist. He changed his major and soon found an area of study for which his talents were better suited.

The Danger of Trying to Live Up To Other People's Expectations

Young people can be put under tremendous pressure by well-meaning parents to pursue particular career paths that are wholly inconsistent with their child's aptitudes and temperament. Many mothers and fathers, whose own lifelong dreams were never realized, are known to have saddled their children with their own unfulfilled career expectations. When this occurs the young person is expected to fulfill a duty that presents an impassable divide between their actual selves and their parent's expectations. Often the results are tragic. The youngster's abilities are often no better suited to the challenges before them than breadsticks are for building bridges. Millions of decent men and women in the workforce perform poorly because they are ill-matched to the jobs they perform and are very unhappy because they don't like their work. One of the best ways of telling whether a person is suited to a particular line is how the experience of performing the work resonates within that person's inner being. Does the person just "like it," or does the person absolutely "love it"? The question you can ask yourself is, "How do I feel about myself doing the work that I am doing?"

We once talked to a thirty-two-year-old landscape designer named Stanley who faced the dilemma of not wanting to disappoint his parents but not wanting to follow the career path they set for him. Stanley went into the family business but deep down he felt it wasn't right for him.

> My father owned a nursery in our town and my brother and I both worked there as teenagers. Dad always thought of himself as more than a nurseryman. He saw himself as a landscape architect and he wanted others to think of him that way too—you know, as someone important that customers would come to for advice and ideas. I think he wanted my brother and me to be landscape architects. We would have lots of people coming in to buy trees and shrubs in early fall and spring months who needed help in laying out their yards. I had an excellent memory for what plants did well in sun or shade. So it fell to me to help our customers with planning how to landscape their yards. I studied botany at our local college and then went to work for a large landscape architectural firm as a designer to get experience.
>
> For the past ten years I have been working as a designer. I am embarrassed to say it but I'm not advancing. Younger people here with much less experience than I have are moving ahead of me. The management likes my attention to detail and wants me to take over the office duties, where I'd be in charge of billings, purchases, keeping track of inventory, things like that. I've been resisting this because I think I'm a better designer than they give me credit for. But you know what? I think I'd really like the office duties better. I just don't want to disappoint Dad.

Here is Stanley, thirty-two years old, stuck in a dead-end job, going nowhere. Why? He's trying to be someone he isn't. Out of respect for his parents, he pictures himself as being a talented designer but in truth he is only mediocre. Younger men and women with more ability are moving ahead of Stanley. When he was a teenager Stanley got it into his head that he was a pretty good designer, and he may have been one for the level he was operating at, helping folks decide where to place trees and shrubs. He knew exactly what conditions were most suitable for each plant species. But this isn't an aesthetic ability. It is the ability of memory, an ability that involves attention to detail. Regardless, once having accepted this inaccurate image of his abilities, Stanley is setting himself up for disappointment as reality catches up with him. By doing this, by tenaciously holding on to a fixed and inaccurate assessment of his aptitudes and talents, Stanley fails the challenge of self-acceptance that life presents to all of us. What is more, he is making himself miserable because of his refusal to accept reality.

Each normal human being has an inner craving to be of some special kind of value, to have worth, and to mean something to somebody. This craving must be met if we are to feel valued, important, worthy of respect. The trick is to satisfy the craving with real accomplishment, by doing well. And the surest way to achieve this goal is by doing those things which we are best able to do. False flattery, an inaccurate assessment of one's talents and abilities, and trying to please others who expect us to be something that we are not are the most common reasons why people slip up in trying to fulfill this basic human need. We are more inclined to listen to outright flattery than we are to stern assessments of our actual performance. We try to please others whose opinions we value and we blunder badly whenever their expectations are inconsistent with our real talents. Worse yet, the deception continues, crowding out the attainment of authentic self-acceptance as we lie to ourselves about our true passions, interests, and talent, so intent are we on pleasing others.

Our advice to Stanley is this: Accept your aesthetic ability for what it is, mediocre. You don't lose value because of what you are not. You gain value for what you are and for how well you cultivate those talents. Too many people get stuck in life by continuing to do those things in the same ways that they have always done them. They fail to grow as persons because they never take a chance by doing something different, something that their heart tells them to try to do. They often resist trying something different because they also fear failing at something unknown to them. It is generally good advice for anyone to allow for their hidden, yet-to-be-discovered abilities to emerge. But these abilities and passions can only reveal themselves if one takes on new challenges or performs old functions in new ways.

Deal with Failure in Healthy Ways

When failure to perform well in one line of work occurs many find the reality too unbearable to stomach. It calls for a healthy level of self-acceptance to handle disappointments. Self-acceptance involves choosing to face oneself as one really is and not giving up on oneself. But not giving up on oneself does not mean keeping going in the same direction. It frequently involves choosing another direction, one in which a person is better suited. To make a well-thought-out change in one's direction does not prevent success and fulfillment but enables it. Yet it is humiliating to admit a failure and to have to abandon an earlier choice of work or job assignment in favor of another one. Many people are humiliated by situations that they need not be. Still, overcoming a sense of humiliation, however real or imagined, is never easy. And many make the mistake of focusing on their feelings of humiliation instead of admitting to them and moving on with their careers in other directions. We make a big mistake whenever we try to fight feelings of humiliation that arise when our performance in a chosen line of work is unsuccessful or unfulfilling. Denial invites unhealthy responses— rationalization, sour grapes, fantasy, and resignation with exaggerated acknowledgements of one's inferiority.

Consider the situation faced by Gene, a thirty-three-year-old golf pro. Here is what he said:

> I learned to play golf from my grandfather when I was five years old. Golf has been in my blood practically all my life. I lettered in golf all four years in high school. I won a golf scholarship to college. Since graduation I tried getting on the pro tour but never made the cuts. I have been teaching golf at country clubs for ten years now, but I'm not doing very well at it. Two clubs let me go because the members didn't think I was giving them what they wanted in lessons. My friends tell me that my techniques are difficult to master and most people don't want to commit themselves to the discipline my methods require. Most just want some pointers so they can clean up one or two parts of their game. Those who do follow my methods find tremendous improvement

but it takes them quite a while to get there. The problem is that people are just too lazy to follow my advice. If they did, they'd be much better players, but they are too lazy.

There are literally millions of people who, like Gene, struggle against disappointment every day as they try to make their mark in the world. Disappointment can be a very good thing or a very bad thing. It all depends on how you react to it. Ought one accept disappointments meekly or face them head-on and forge ahead in the same direction? Sometimes disappointment helps us realize that what we tried was foolish or ill-conceived. At other times it makes sense to see defeat as just a bump on the road to success making us stronger, more determined. Regardless of which way makes the most sense, we ought to view disappointment as the workings of our inner voice. Do we hear it speak? Or do we rationalize, as Gene does, to cover up our failures?

Facing defeat is not an easy thing to do. A fragile ego wants us to conclude that the failure was not ours but someone else's doing. We do not want to lose face. We fear ridicule. This is how our egos prevent us from admitting our disappointments and moving on. Consider the case of Krista, who had it built into her mind from a very early age that she was an excellent piano player. Her family, her friends, her teachers believed that Krista needed encouragement, so whenever she played they praised her efforts with complimentary bravos. But the sad truth was that, despite all she had heard and despite her love of music, Krista was not all that good. The truth was that she was an above average, high school-level musician, nothing more. So, when she auditioned as part of the admission process to a good conservatory of music and got turned down, Krista was crushed.

Did she accept the truth—that piano playing was not the talent with which she could best distinguish herself? Not Krista. Her fragile ego told her that she was being cheated out of what was rightfully hers. As a consequence, Krista still holds on to her high opinion of her self. She keeps her dreams of becoming an acclaimed musician alive through what's known as fantasy. In her mind she is right, the others are wrong. She convinces herself that she just had an off day when she performed her audition. In her mind, those who judged her didn't know enough about music to form a valid opinion of her musical talents. But these words of self-assurance alone are an insufficient balm for the wound

Krista received. Her hurt has now turned into anger and her anger has turned into a desire for revenge—she wants to rid the world of people like those who judged her as being a mediocre pianist. Her aim has now turned from playing the piano to finding ways to even the score. The more she moves in this direction, the more she becomes an even greater enemy of herself. She tells others about how incompetent and unfair those who judged her were, and, in so doing, she burns the bridges that might connect her to opportunities for performing.

How to Live Effectively with an Inferior or Unlovely Element in Your Nature

Every normal person wants to feel good about him- or herself. It is easy to accept compliments on our successes and to have self-confidence because of our strengths. But feeling too secure because of one's strengths and superiorities can prove disastrous. It is a dangerous half-truth that we are made great by our superior abilities and destroyed by our inferior ones. History is rich in examples of persons who have been spoiled by the same strengths that earlier led to their successes and achievements. When relied upon too heavily the strength a person skillfully uses to win acclaim in one realm can easily lead to their ruin in another. The intellect a leader uses, for example, to outwit an adversary is frequently found to be the source of an unbearable attitude of superiority that colleagues and immediate subordinates cannot abide. He wraps his mind's powers around the facts of a situation to formulate a winning strategy but the capabilities of his heart remain underdeveloped and never bring him to understand and appreciate the strong feelings and emotions of those who are called upon to execute the strategy. Is it any wonder, then, that brilliant plans are frequently executed so poorly? The smartest person, gifted with superior ability, frequently falls on his own sword. "He might be a brilliant person," we hear people say about a coworker, "but who can stand to be around him?"

When in the course of life's trials we encounter failure we are at the same time given a great opportunity: we can learn about the personal deficiency, the weakness that led to our failure. Never underestimate the value of these kinds of lessons. But also be aware of the challenge they pose. Healthy self-acceptance involves facing these inferiorities in all their reality. This is neither easy nor common. Such circumstances naturally throw us into a position of defensiveness, where we either deny or downplay the importance of our deficiency. We become resentful, fearful, threatened, humiliated. From these strong emotions spring all kinds of unhealthy and unhelpful responses: excuse-making, blaming of others, nervous disorders, dejection. Some people even retreat into a state of resignation. They give up hope of ever amounting to anything and announce their inferiority in exaggerated terms. It becomes the perfect excuse; they use it to run away to escape any further humiliation. What initially presented itself as a minor shortcoming, one that might have been dealt with constructively, has now turned into a more complicated cluster of psychological impediments. Now these new problems must be sorted out and resolved before any positive steps can be taken to repair the initial difficulty.

Healthy self-acceptance involves acknowledging a weakness and dealing with it as well as with the unpleasant emotions that arise from finding the deficiency.

> I feel humiliated about the failure to perform well because of my tendency to ignore important details. I know that in my haste to finish an assignment I do not pay as much attention to the little things that I ought to consider. Sometimes, this tendency lands me in hot water.

These are the words of a person who is honestly facing a shortcoming and who is also acknowledging the emotions that accompany the failure it caused. They portray a healthy level of self-acceptance. This person makes real to his self what he has done, the deficiency behind it, and how he feels. It is only when we acknowledge our actions and feelings as they really are, that we put ourselves into a position to do something about them and to change for the better.

It is true that a deficiency can sometimes be a positive stimulus. We all admire those who have turned some shaming inferior quality into a superlative strength and achieved eminence from it. But these situations are few. In most situations other approaches are more realistic. We might all like to see ourselves in the same category of excellence as a Mercedes or Lexus automobile but in reality we are really more like the simple Jeep in terms of our talents. Yet we do well to keep in mind that the Jeep is equipped to get people to places where the high-priced luxury cars could never maneuver. To use one's distinctive abilities is a positive thing, even though they may be more common and less impressive than those of others.

Another healthy approach for handling an embarrassing inferiority is to convert it into a useful instrument for achieving something good. Some of the most splendid accomplishments known have been made by those who earlier struggled with some inferiority. Such struggles give people the insight, sympathy, and understanding needed to accomplish amazing feats. In a book compiled by Steve Young called *Great Failures of the Extremely Successful*, a man named Joseph Batory tells of how his embarrassing inferiority laid the groundwork for a career of public service, saving young people from going bad. Reared in a very tough and very Italian South Philadelphia neighborhood, gang members bullied Joseph terribly. He was small and quiet and his father told him not to "rock the boat" and to avoid confrontations. For Joey Batory going to school was a terrifying experience. The tougher boys knocked his books out of his hands, broke into his locker, and smacked him around on the school bus. Whenever he saw a group of kids coming, Joey would run away in fear. "I was fearful all the time," he said. "I ended up crying in my room every night." Later and in his adult years Batory turned what he had learned about fear and tough neighborhoods into useful guidelines for saving other kids from the devastating ills of inner-city life—drugs, violence, crime. He rose to become a school superintendent in Upper Darby, one of the most diverse and successful districts in the country. His book *Yo! Joey!* has become a guide for educators across the country.

We knew a very smart man named John who worked for a mining company many years ago. He was the kind of person who could do very good work as long as he worked alone. But put John around other people for long and he had a way of irritating them. This is a fairly common occurrence when someone has a very clear idea as to how things ought to be done and insists on following a carefully thought-out, precise process for accomplishing jobs. John was quick to spot whatever it was that was causing a mechanical problem and he knew exactly how to fix it. He was highly reliable and trustworthy but he did not suffer fools easily. Management had to learn how to use John for his strengths. What might have been the right job assignment for other bright people, like a Margaret or a James, was not the right assignment for John. They made a special position for John, general foreman of maintenance. He didn't manage anyone directly, but he did have authority to assign people to specific jobs. Day after day, John roamed the operation finding mechanical problems and breakdowns that needed attention, and he was just the right person to fix them—which he did with great distinction.

Management recognized John's strengths and his limitations. To get the most out of his good qualities, they designed a position where his assets would be best put to service without the handicap of being spoiled by his limitations. There is a useful lesson for all of us in this example. Every person receives both distinctive and restrictive endowments. It is up to us to figure out what can best be made of them. Julia might have a knack for detail but little in the way of originality. Ashley may be good when it comes to creating beautiful displays and designs but not know what time of day it is and have trouble managing her schedule. To envy others for their talents does no good and to imitate someone we admire is suicidal. We are all different and it's up to each of us to make the best of what we've got. And when we know we have some limitation or weakness, it shows good judgment to work around it, to avoid putting the weakness into situations where it might cause us to fail. And so, if I know that I have a short fuse then it does not make good sense to allow myself to get into situations where that fuse might be ignited.

Handle Strong Emotions Effectively

Imagine how you might feel if you were asked to make a speech before an important body of higher-ups in your organization. Most people would be scared. Indeed, surveys show that the number one fear people have is to make a speech in public. Fear. It is a strong emotion. There are all kinds of emotions people experience in the workplace. A person does a dumb thing and feels embarrassed about it. Another person cannot stand a particular coworker and becomes highly irritated when the two have to interact. Still another person finds herself becoming angry about her pay and work schedule. Anger, fear, embarrassment, resentment, humiliation—these are some of the typical negative emotions everyone experiences both at and away from the workplace.

We don't like our negative emotions. They are difficult to handle and most of us would prefer to keep them in their place and escape their terrorizing effects. But we can't. They are alive and strong, and they menace us at every turn. What to do? Here's what a man named Joe did when he recognized his fear of having to perform a difficult assignment that he had never undertaken before. Joe feared that he'd bungle the job and that the others who relied on his work would ridicule him for it. So, there he was, faced both with a difficult job to do and a deep-seated fear of failure. Joe did a very wise thing. Paradoxically, it was the exact opposite of what most people think makes good sense. Instead of thinking that he could rise above his fear by suppressing it, by saying to himself, "This fear I have is just in my head and I can defeat it," Joe looked at his fear directly. He dealt with it head-on before tackling the tough assignment. Instead of fighting or denying his feeling, Joe accepted its existence. He admitted to himself that his fear was alive and strong. Inside, he felt, "I may have this fear in me but this fear is not me. I am something more than this fear. I may be afraid but that is no reason for me to try to escape this fear."

Joe recognized correctly that a person cannot live or work effectively if fears, and other strong emotions for that matter, are ignored. They have to be faced and dealt with in a forthright, honest way. And this is exactly what he did: he thought to himself, "What's the worst thing that could happen if I blow this assignment?" He invited his fear to tell him straight out what it had in store for him if the worst possible consequence came about. When a person allows herself to accept a negative feeling she is able to let go of it. When she does this her fear does not have control of her, she has control of it. Once the fear has had its say, the fear will then melt away.

Self-acceptance involves the willingness to experience all that we think, feel, desire, have done, and are. It is being present in the reality of our selves, our emotions, our thoughts and our behavior. We are always stronger whenever we choose not to fight reality, but to accept it head-on, honestly and completely. And if in the process of dealing with strong emotions, one finds himself fighting or trying to block it, the smartest thing to do is to admit that he is doing that too, blocking and fighting the emotion. You cannot overcome a negative emotion if you deny having it in the first place. Accept its existence, absorb it, contemplate it, and understand it. That done, the negative emotion will, like a naughty child after having "acted up," tire and subside into the background. Now you can get to work on what needs doing.

SHARPEN YOUR THINKING SKILLS

See Beyond the Obvious, Pay Attention to Your Surroundings, Anticipate Consequences and Outcomes

"You may be only a speck traveling across the landscape but you'd better be a speck that thinks."

Susan Butcher, Iditarod winner 1986–1988 and 1990

Once, as a group of foremen were exchanging work stories, one of them asked a question: "What was the dumbest thing you ever saw an employee do?" The supervisors there shared numerous examples but the following tale topped them all. The foreman who told this story worked in a warehouse. "We had just received several orders of parts and they needed to be placed in storage bins," he said. "I asked a new man to stack them on the shelves that ran floor to ceiling along a wall of our building. To get items to the upper shelves he would need to place them in a basket and hoist it to the right height. A rope, tied to the basket, ran through a pulley up above. He was to raise the basket filled with parts and then climb up a ladder and unload them on the shelves above. The man proceeded with the assigned task. He loaded the basket with parts and raised it to a height where he could take them out for shelving. Then, not knowing what to do with the end of the rope he held, the man tied it to his belt and climbed the ladder. Once he got to the top of the ladder, the basket was no longer there—no parts. Bewildered, he looked around and then down. There, sitting on the ground, he spotted the basket. So, he climbed down the ladder to get it. But once back down on the ground the basket wasn't there either.

Now he was completely baffled. He looked up and there it was—high above, dangling from the overhead pulley."

This story illustrates the importance of thinking. Let your brain rest for just a moment and you can end up doing dumb things and look foolish. Allow your mind to wander off as you proceed about your business and an unexpected accident can claim an eye, a hand or an arm, or even your life. Forget momentarily to do what you are supposed to be doing and a sale can be lost, a product could be ruined in production, a defect might slip past undetected. Yes, keeping your mind engaged and alert is vital not just to your work performance but also to your well-being. Billions of dollars are made or lost in the world of work every year depending on whether people were thinking clearly and skillfully or were not thinking at all.

The Value of a Thinking Employee

Every employer knows that a thinking employee is a valued asset. These are the individuals who come up with better methods, see mistakes and fix them before they grow large and costly, identify safer and more productive ways of getting work accomplished, and make the work environment alive and exciting with new ideas. There may be things that some working people do over and over—we're all familiar with assembly-line work—but many other tasks are unique and require a fair amount of "figuring out" on the spot. Those who can think for themselves and gauge what to do on their own are highly desirable. Smart, quick-thinking employees, men and women who have the capacity to decide what needs doing and how to do it spell the difference between good outcomes with happy endings and constant disasters.

It is always good advice to keep your wits about you. This means paying attention to what's happening and to what might happen. We learned of an incident that took place in Plymouth, Wisconsin, that illustrates this important idea. A man named Christopher Ondercin, twenty, was working the next to last day of a summer job at his local Wal-Mart, before returning to college for the fall semester. Earlier, Christopher had learned from an employee at another store that two men were using fake credit cards to buy gift cards. Little did he realize it at the time but he was about to confront these men himself. A little past lunchtime that day, one of these men stood before Ondercin asking to buy gift cards. Christopher was immediately suspicious. To stall for time he lied to the man, telling him that he was new and that he did not know how to process that kind of transaction. Christopher got his supervisor to handle the transaction. In the meantime he went out to the parking lot, wrote down the license plate of the man's vehicle and gave a description of the men and their vehicle to police. A short distance away, police arrested Shahir Mahmoud, forty-eight, of Sunnyside, New York. His accomplice, Youness Attobi, thirty-eight, of Cincinnati was apprehended later. The pair was charged with ten counts of possession of a counterfeit credit card. A further search of their van revealed more than two hundred fake credit cards, false New York driver's licenses, seven Wal-Mart gift cards in denominations between $500 and $800, and other items.

Sometimes an employee demonstrates his value not by doing his work well but by figuring out quickly what the smart thing is and doing it straightaway. We read a news account of something like this that occurred in Lester-Prairie, Minnesota. There the quick actions of an employee from Treasure Hunt Antiques saved six customers and himself from serious injury. At around 4:30 on a June afternoon a truck driver from Joel Hilgers Trucking of Waconia came into the antique shop. Todd Pruden was on duty. The driver told Pruden that his truck had just knocked over an electrical pole causing a live wire to fall across a large propane tank located near the front corner of their building. The hose connected to the tank had a minor leak in it. Pruden was aware of the leaking hose, which was scheduled to be repaired. Pruden calmly explained the dangerous situation to his customers and they left immediately while local firefighters were notified. The firefighters secured the area so no one would pull into the lot. Xcel Energy sent a crew that arrived within the hour. They cut the cable, repaired the leak, and straightened the pole, since it hadn't been damaged.

Recently, I (Charles) received a cookbook written by a longtime friend. Having enjoyed many good meals at this friend's home, I decided to put the book to good use. I thumbed through its pages and decided to prepare one of the most appealing recipes, Chinese pork in brown sauce. I then made a list of the ingredients and went to my local grocer to buy the needed items. After checking out and returning home with my purchases, I realized that the new bag boy, Eric, had his own system for bagging groceries. Eric obviously thought about the customer by the way in which he sorted items into separate plastic grocery bags: meat was double-wrapped to prevent messy seepages onto other items and placed in a separate bag. Noodles and rice were placed in another bag. Bay leaves, Hoisin sauce, canned tomatoes, soy sauce, sesame seed oil all went into another bag. Carrots, bok choy, and green onions were in still another bag. The next time I saw Eric, I asked him about his methods. "Oh yes," he said with a bright smile. "I do that on purpose. I know what happens when people get home and start putting their groceries away. The dry items like rice and noodles will go into a cupboard. Vegetables and meats will be stored in a refrigerator. My system makes the unpacking convenient." Employers love to have people like Eric working for them. They please customers, and don't make mistakes. And perhaps, just perhaps, their good ideas and example might rub off on other employees.

Live Consciously

How many people have you seen going through their workdays and driving on the streets and highways with their consciousness disengaged? Maybe you have been one of them. It is wise to keep in mind that as human beings we have the power to choose whether to seek awareness of our surroundings or to disengage our minds and tune out what's around us. We can care and keep our brains in gear or we can shrug our shoulders and take an "I don't care" attitude. Of course the more difficult path is the one that involves maintaining your alertness.

Even though people are unequal in terms of intelligence—some are more gifted intellectually than others—we all have the same capacity to be aware of our surroundings. Being conscious of what's going on around us is not a matter of raw intellect. It is not intelligence that's needed, it is consciousness. You have probably known some very intelligent people who have done some very foolish things. Afterward, these people would admit privately that their trouble arose because they had their level of consciousness turned down low or off entirely. Living consciously involves being aware of everything that's going on. It means being alert. It means noticing what it is that demands that we act in one way or another. And it means that we alter our behavior according to what we see, feel, hear, and know to be true.

We came across a very sad story about a man described in an OSHA accident report who failed to engage his consciousness as he ought. This employee worked on a construction site and apparently wanted to get from where he was to another spot. He didn't consider the danger that lay in the path he chose to take. As a result he was crushed to death by a backhoe when he tried to walk between it and a concrete wall. A contractor was operating the backhoe but didn't see this man because he approached from the operator's blind side. The contractor was unaware of his presence. When the operator swung the backhoe around, its superstructure (the section of the backhoe containing the engine positioned behind the operator) hit the victim, crushing him against a concrete wall.

Living consciously also means paying attention to what we call our "Danger, alert!" signals. Most people at one time or another make themselves their own worst enemy when they ignore what their inner feelings are telling them is dangerous. The "Danger, alert!" inner feeling that a laborer experiences when working with power tools and the accompanying fear sensation that comes with it are healthy signs that the consciousness level detects something worth respecting. Unsafe feelings are the mind's way of saying to us, "Watch out. Be careful. Get away. Don't do it." Anyone who has stood near a passing train traveling at a high rate of speed knows the feeling of power and danger that comes from such an experience. When we hear of people who drive across railroad tracks to beat out a passing train, we know that these foolish people have ignored their "danger, alert!" sensations— and some do so at the cost of their lives.

The laborer who says, "I know, for safety reasons, that I should disconnect the power source of this piece of equipment before working on it," but chooses not to, goes against what her consciousness is trying to tell her: "Danger, alert!" Our consciousness exists to protect us and move us and those around us away from dangers and toward smarter choices. Whenever we ignore it, refusing to allow a power that makes us more human, and, presumably, superior to other living creatures, we become our own worst enemy. The great French philosopher, mathematician, and physicist, Blaise Pascal (1623–1662), once observed, "Man is obviously made for thinking. Therein lies all his dignity and his merit; and his whole duty is to think, as he ought."

The Dangers of Daydreaming

Stay focused. Keep your mind alert to what's going on. Good advice, but it is difficult to follow, particularly during tense and difficult times at work. Nonetheless, your alertness is always necessary for safe and quality performance. At night, of course, we dream while we sleep. This serves a vital function for our mental health. In our sleep, dreams relieve the pressures of our busy lives. We all dream away the daily anxieties that plague us—the unspoken fears, passions, and lusts that would torment and embarrass us if we confronted them in our waking hours. But unlike dreaming, which is therapeutic, there is daydreaming, which is something else entirely. Daydreaming is an escape. While the body is in one place, the daydreaming mind wanders somewhere else. It takes us from the unpleasantness and the unbearable realities of the immediate and into a realm of make-believe reverie. Daydreaming is a process that we allow to happen. It takes us away from what we are doing and transports us mentally to where we would prefer to be, to what we want to be, or to what we wish we were doing.

As a young man, I (Tom) did what anyone who needs money for college would do, I got a job. Uneducated and unskilled at the time, the best job I could get was washing city buses at the municipal garage. Dirty from their daily rounds, the buses needed to be hosed down, scrubbed clean, rinsed, and wiped dry before being sent out the next morning. This part of the job was fun. Portland's summers are sometimes hot, and using a water hose is good, clean—and cooling—fun. The part of my job that wasn't fun was tire changing. This was a necessary but difficult and dirty aspect of the work. It required patience, muscle power, attention to detail, getting dirty, and dealing with frustration and anger when things didn't go smoothly, which they frequently didn't. It was here, in the midst of this part of the job—the dirty, unpleasant, frustrating part—that I found my thoughts moving away from the dirt and heat and difficulties at hand. I began to daydream. It's something every normal person is prone to do—to slip away from unpleasant work and into more pleasing longings and circumstances. This occurs so naturally that we scarcely recognize it is happening to us. You can easily imagine me at the time. I am twenty years old. It is a warm summer's night and I am wrestling a large, uncooperative wheel off a bus. The wheel is dirty, heavy, and stuck to the bolts that hold in on the bus axle. I have to change the tire that's mounted on it, something that will require more muscle power, more sweat, more patience. My girlfriend is waiting impatiently for me to take her on a date later that night. I want to leave work but know that I cannot do that. I can make myself stay where the work is but my mind wants to wander away from the reality of the unpleasant and into the realm of the imagination.

It is at such moments that one's attention is likely to move away from the difficult and travel into the realm of what's more pleasant to think about. It is here, when our thoughts are far away from the work at hand, that we are most vulnerable to accidents and mistakes. Now it is at these times that we make ourselves our number one enemy. The smart thing to do is to fight our tendency to daydream. Sure, we want to escape mentally from the work at hand, to avoid the unpleasant, dirty, difficult work we must do. But remember this: it is when we are not paying close enough attention to details that errors are missed and missteps occur. Here we allow our wandering minds to lead us into more trouble. When we choose not to daydream, we keep our minds focused on what we are actually doing, on what we should be doing—and then we do those things better and more safely.

See Individual Parts and the Whole in Their "Togetherness"

Let's examine something that we've all noticed about ourselves and others. Some of us are more oriented to looking at things as total entities—the big picture. Others of us tend to be more detail-oriented—we see the individual parts and are keen on examining each part of a whole in great depth. The old question "Do you see the trees or the forest?" captures the essence of the distinction between the big picture and the detail-oriented ways of perceiving. But it is worth our while to press the issue further: What ought one pay attention to—the big picture, the forest, or the details, the individual trees? The view of the person who sees only the big picture, the forest, lacks clarification and precision. The person who sees only the details, the individual trees, lacks an understanding of what they mean as a whole and how they combine to form something collectively that's larger than what they are individually. These simple ideas are extraordinarily useful in helping us to raise our levels of consciousness. The ideal is to strive to see both the details and the big picture. We call this "seeing things in their togetherness."

Seeing both the individual parts and the whole, together, is not a new idea. Immanual Kant (1724–1804), the famous German philosopher, stated in his books that the human mind is fashioned by the Divine to see things *together*. Centuries earlier, in Greece, Plato wrote of the human mind as possessing powers of unifying energy—an energy that can see and understand the one-in-the-many, the particular, and the universal, the whole, together. Our minds, Plato thought, are more fully developed when we elevate our powers of awareness, our consciousness, to see things in their togetherness, both the parts and the whole.

These abstract ideas can be of the greatest practical value to anyone. The person who masters details and is not defeated by trying to understand them will get all the small, but necessary steps correct that spell the difference between a quality job and a sloppily performed one. We know a superb craftsman who builds museum-quality furniture styled after the eighteenth-century masters. Watch him working in his shop and you'll observe a person paying extraordinary attention to detail— every angle is measured before and after being cut, machine setups are checked for accuracy using scrap pieces, and finer adjustments, if necessary, are made before actual cuts are performed on actual parts. But this craftsman's concerns are not solely with details. Always the parts are judged in relationship to the whole and the abiding criterion is, "Do the parts fit aesthetically with the whole piece? Is the part too wide, too narrow? Is the angle or curve too sharp or not sharp enough?"

Years ago, when I (Tom) was fourteen years old and living in Portland, Oregon, I learned, firsthand, why seeing the parts and the whole together is essential to success. Hired to wash dishes at the Bohemian Restaurant in downtown Portland, I worked under the constant and careful direction of the restaurant's owner, George O'Neil. O'Neil's restaurant was filled to capacity at lunchtime with discerning diners who munched on its sumptuous bread sticks and topped off their meals with delicious pastries. George O'Neil served top-quality meals to his customers, giving them excellent service. He had an eye for detail: everything had to be just so and he was constantly watching that it was—chairs were wiped clean, crumbs swept off counters and floors, and napkins were always folded carefully.

One day, as I scoured bread pans in the basement of the bakery, I looked up to see George standing beside me, observing me as I scrubbed away. Even the washing of pans in which breads, pies, tortes, cobblers, and cakes were baked concerned George. He knew that spick-and-span baking pans are one of the many keys to quality bakery products. George dipped his hands into the hot soapy water and took hold of the scrub brush I was using and showed me how to get into the deepest corners of the pan. He was not about to leave the quality of pots and pans washing to the haphazard and inexperienced eye of a fourteen-year-old boy. His role was to teach each employee how to perform his or her individual tasks at a level that would make his restaurant what he wanted it to be as a whole: providing each customer with a first-rate dining experience. George knew that the reputation of his Bohemian Restaurant depended on the totality of the seemingly smallest things—the filling of salt and pepper shakers, the cleanliness of remote corners of each room, the proper laundering of napkins and tablecloths. George's eyes took in everything and his mind told him if things were going well. He watched the plates of his customers after they had finished their meals. If they liked what he served, it was eaten; he wanted to see plates eaten clean. And he also watched his cash register carefully, usually ringing up sales himself. Keeping eaters satisfied with good meals was his business and his passion. And he knew that profits came when people liked what he served. So he focused his attention on the tiniest aspects and the final results—together!

Think About How to Be More Productive

Many years ago, at a forest-products company in Montana, a man named Clarence ran a small department of fifteen people called the "cut up" department. These employees were responsible for sawing and milling wood moldings—the long, figured pieces of wood that are nailed to walls around doors and windows. They are baseboards, crown moldings, chair rails, wainscoting, and the like. During a supervisory management course Clarence heard about the effects goal-setting can have on productivity and motivation. The idea was that people are more highly motivated when they are working toward clear-cut goals and when they can see their progress toward meeting those targets. Clarence thought he'd give this idea a try. He began by telling his people about the importance of having work goals, production output targets. At first they didn't quite know what to think of all this goal-setting stuff he was telling them; but they liked Clarence, so they went along with him on it.

Clarence thought of the best days his workers had turning out molding and how much they had produced on the average days. He looked for a target that would not be so high that his people would laugh at him but not so low that there would be no challenge to it. After considering the problem for a few days Clarence announced a target: 17,000 lineal feet of moldings would be produced per shift. He posted the target amount on a bulletin board. At the end of their first day, his group produced 14 percent below the daily goal. Not good, but not too bad either. The next few days showed improvement. On the last day of the first week his unit was only 2.9 percent off the expected mark. The challenge caught on with the employees. And then, halfway into the following week his people surprised him and themselves when they surpassed the 17,000 lineal feet mark by 1.5 percent. Morale and motivation turned upward. Interest in the work shot upward. Better methods began to be the topic of lunch- and breaktime chatter. "Are we going to make our target today?" they would ask Clarence. After a few weeks' time, the employees began setting their own goals and they implemented productivity improvements too. They also started helping each other out. If one person was having a bad day, feeling lousy or ill, the others would pick up the slack.

Think About Those Who Depend on What You Do—Customers

Employees who "sleepwalk" through their workdays endanger the reputation of their employer and sometimes those who depend on their expertise to get things done right. Imagine that you own a jet boat—one that's powered by an engine that sucks water in and shoots it out so you can traverse rocky waterways that would otherwise stop the typical outboard engine's rotating propeller. The owner of one of these boats had his repaired at Sears Marina in Anchorage, Alaska, in preparation for a day of salmon fishing. A few hours drive north of Anchorage, the owner launched his boat in the Susitna River, known in the area as the "Big Su." The Susitna is a glacial river with many channels, islands, and logjams. It is large, fast-moving, and ice cold. After running downstream a few miles something suddenly went wrong with the boat's engine. A bearing in the jet unit froze, causing the motor to seize. Now the boat was helpless, completely without power. Like an awkward raft the boat drifted sideways, out of control, with water coming within inches of pouring over the upstream side of the boat. Down the river it floated until it piled into a logjam where it almost capsized. The owner used an axe to break free. A careless service technician, sleepwalking through his day's work had neglected to pack the bearing with grease before installing it. This mindless oversight by a technician could easily have resulted in a man's death. Fortunately no one drowned and the damaged boat was eventually recovered.

Think About Avoiding Danger

It is always good advice to be alert to dangers—to know what might possibly go wrong. This way one can protect himself by keeping out of harm's way. Sometime ago two men who worked for a siding company were sent to a farmhouse to install aluminum siding. Before they could attach siding to one side of the house it became necessary to remove a thirty-six-foot-tall metal pole CB antenna. This was something they had done before. But what they didn't take into consideration was the high-voltage power line nearby. One of the men stood on a metal pickboard between two ladders and unfastened the antenna at the top of the house. The other man, who was standing on the ground, took the antenna to lay it down in the yard. The antenna made electrical contact with a 7,200-volt power transmission line thirty feet from the house and twenty-three feet above the ground. The employee handling the antenna received a fatal shock and the other employee, on the metal pick, a minor shock.

Sometimes people get so focused on what they have to do that they forget to consider what's going on around themselves that might be important. In the case of the aluminum siding installers, these men neglected the danger posed by the power line nearby. In another situation that we learned about, a construction worker was so focused on shooting nails into plywood using a powder-activated nail gun that he accidentally killed a carpenter apprentice working a short distance away. The tool operator, while attempting to anchor a plywood form in preparation for pouring a concrete wall, fired the gun, causing the nail to pass through the hallow wall and into the head of the victim.

All kinds of dangers exist in the workplace that should be seen for what they are. These dangers could be physical conditions that might lead to a personal injury or they could be human relations tragedies waiting to happen. For example, an overly sensitive person might easily take offense at an offhand remark innocently made by a coworker. As with physical dangers, emotional dangers might easily be avoided by not being so focused on the job itself that one fails to recognize the feelings of others as well.

Think About the "Bottom Line"

Employees at all levels of every imaginable enterprise, be it a profit or a nonprofit entity, have shown themselves capable of finding ways to produce more value for less cost. By thinking, they find better ways to create more value. These people have what we call a *bottom-line* mentality. A bottom-line mentality is simply the perspective of trying to find ways of creating more value per resource. All too frequently, people get caught up in the routine of unthinking habit, doing the same things in the same ways year after year. This is boring and ultimately destructive as minds harden and refuse to accept superior methods. As a consequence, organizations populated by these kinds of employees wither while more progressive, rival firms pass them by.

"We moved from written orders and invoices twenty years ago to telephone and FAX machines," one store owner told us. "Why do we need to switch to Internet and electronic banking services now?" This remark is typical of the kind of thinking that plagues many people in workplaces across the country. These are the very people and organizations that will soon be put out of business by more savvy rivals who continue to rethink the ways they conduct business. In every shop and office space across the land there are possibilities for boosting bottom-line results. Those who shut their minds to these possibilities and continue along the path of unthinking habit not only die mentally but also find their work boring and unfulfilling. They make themselves less human, their work less interesting, and their organizations less competitive.

A friend of ours named Doug Smith from Cincinnati told us about his experiences when he was an area general manager for GTE in Atlanta. Doug was plagued with the problem of lost revenues when good sales representatives left for other positions. Supervising a department of twenty-one sales reps, Doug found himself always having to train new people for recently vacated positions. It took him at least two to three months to get them up to speed. Turnover was part of the environment. When an experienced rep left, the sales in that rep's territory would slip dramatically until a well-trained replacement could take over. The usual practice was to request another hire and begin training the new person. Doug had a better idea and he evaluated its possibilities against the impact it would have on what really mattered to GTE, the bottom line. Why not have a twenty-second person in the department, one who would be in training? It would cost Doug's department a bit more for this person's base pay but when an experienced sales rep left, the drop-off in sales in that rep's area would not suffer, because a well-trained replacement was ready to take over immediately. While it cost more to have a ready replacement, the additional outlay was more than covered because sales were not lost. Doug Smith's idea worked and GTE adopted it throughout its sales organization nationwide.

It is clearly true that what people think about matters, because it affects their behavior. It is also true that what people focus their thoughts upon are those things that get evaluated. There is an old saying that, "what gets inspected get respected." The truth of this statement was illustrated recently by an experience a former student told me (Charles) about. After graduating over twenty-eight years ago, a man named John stopped by earlier this week to renew ties. He had been a student in one of my classes and since then he has kept in touch over the years through Christmas cards. Now, fifty years old and financially successful, he was back on campus to share some of the many experiences he had in the world of business. He told me about a firm in which he had once served as financial officer. This company was in the field of high technology; its principal owners were scientific types who knew their products and the technology behind them. But they were not so knowledgeable about business matters—profits, cash flows, and the like. John had an idea for helping this organization to boost its financial performance. He and those who were responsible for making compensation decisions established a performance reward system, tying raises and bonuses to financial performance measures, such as return on assets, cash flows, productivity of capital. It worked. Within a year's time this firm, which had barely earned enough to keep going and was deep in debt now churned out record-level profits and produced healthy cash flows. The point is that by getting employees to pay attention to the bottom line, the firm's financial performance skyrocketed.

Think Your Way Out of Problems Using Principles You Already Know

A good rule to follow when it appears that you are beaten by an insurmountable obstacle is to consider every possible way around it.

Let your imagination soar. Too often our imaginations remain mired in the web of past routines. We fail, frustrated, not because no way out exists but because we are unable to find a good way out of our difficulty. To find a way out, it is advisable to try to switch gears mentally to consider solutions outside the conventional. Ask yourself: Is there any other possible way around this problem?

Long ago a famous wood finisher named George Frank demonstrated this very concept—the ability to think his way out of what looked like an impossible situation. Since there was no work for him in his native Hungary right after World War I, George traveled to Paris in search of a brighter future. Already, he was a full-fledged cabinet maker and a master of stains and finishes. In 1924, George arrived at the French capital. His first job was painting the Eiffel Tower, but the heights and dangers of working high above the ground didn't agree with him and he quit. His next job was with Ferdinand Schnitzspan, who owned a wood-finishing shop. Customers could not pronounce Schnitzspan's name, so they simply called him Fernan. His employees addressed the master as "Patron."

France's economy was beginning to take off in the years following World War I, and there was plenty of work. The Banque de France was expanding rapidly too; it was Fernan's best customer. His shop had the contract to finish the oak woodwork for the bank's newly opening branches. In June, Fernan's men shipped off all the woodwork for the bank's branch in Lisieux, which was scheduled to open on July 16. Midway through the second week of July bad news arrived at Fernan's shop. He had made a serious error: all the woodwork was stained too light. The bank's architect refused to accept it. A full-blown crisis swept over the busy shop. Fernan and his men would have to travel to Lisieux immediately and work round the clock to darken the oak woodwork before the branch's planned opening. All other work would have to wait.

Fernan and six of his best men squeezed into a car, along with all their needed materials, and set out for Lisieux. Upon entering the bank, their error was obvious. Correcting their mistake would be an enormous undertaking. Even if they worked twenty-four hours a day, their best estimate was that the job would take at least fifteen days to complete. They thought and thought. What could they do to speed up the job? Every suggestion contemplated led to the same conclusion: it would be impossible to complete the restaining job in time.

As Fernan and his trusted men discussed one idea after another, tension mounted. Failure was staring them in the face. George Frank kept his mouth shut. After all, he was the youngest and least experienced. But his mind raced ahead—what could cause oak to darken? What did he know about the coloring of wood that just might help? Then an idea sprang into his head. George touched Fernan's sleeve and said, "Patron, I think I can do the job by tomorrow night."

They all looked at him in disbelief. This was not a time to be joking. Then George explained his idea. It was plainly evident that the time required to restain the oak, using conventional methods of rubbing and restaining, applying the new finish in the usual way, would simply take too long. But what about creating a gas? George knew that ammonia in a strong enough concentration will darken wood—a process called fuming. If they could make a great cloud of ammonia gas, there was a fair chance that it would penetrate the finish and react with the tannic acid in the oak, darkening it.

The men sealed off the room, closing the doors and windows and putting rags in all the cracks. They then fashioned thirty simple alcohol burners. Each burner consisted of a ten-inch square board with three nails driven in it. At the center of the nails they set a dish containing half a pint of alcohol. Then they placed a bucket of liquid ammonia on the nails. That done and arranged throughout the bank, the men scurried about, wet towels over their faces, lighting the alcohol burners. They left the lights on so they could see from outside what was happening. As the burners caused the liquid ammonia to boil a thick cloud of gas developed—it was too dense to see what was happening. Fernan and his men would just have to wait. Suspense ran high. No one could sleep. They played cards, drank apple brandy, and waited. Every once in a while someone would go out to check on what was happening but every time they came back with the same news: it wasn't possible to tell. They would have to wait till morning to find out.

The next afternoon the bank's architect arrived and peered through a window. They all waited anxiously, wondering what his verdict would be. Then, he smiled and nodded approvingly. The ammonia gas had done its work; the oak had been darkened. The bank could open on schedule.

A good rule to follow when you are confronted with a difficult problem is to create a list of every possible fact or reality about the situation that comes to mind. This is precisely what George Frank did.

He knew that the color of the wood was not dark enough to please the client. What might be done to darken it? Obviously a darker stain could be used but that would be difficult because a clear top coat covered what was on the wood already. Then George Frank remembered a basic fact—ammonia gas would darken wood and it could penetrate through the top coat to do it. This example gives us a model to follow for our own thinking when facing difficult problems: Ask yourself, "Is there any other way to accomplish your purpose?"

We know of a woman named Patty who works as a sales rep for a firm that makes contact lenses. She markets these lenses to optometrists and ophthalmologists who, in turn, prescribe and sell them to their patients. Patty thought it might make sense to get information about her products directly to potential customers. The question she faced was how to do that? Then an idea entered her mind. She remembered that when she got her last driver's license she had to take an eye exam, and because she wore prescription lenses to see properly that fact was noted on her license. She also knew that driver-license information is in the public domain. She or anyone else could access it. Here was the answer she sought: names and addresses of individuals who wore corrective lenses for their vision.

Anticipate Consequences

Like strong headlights on an automobile that illuminate what's on the road ahead, a forward-anticipating mind can help us steer around dangers and reach our goals safely. Anticipate the consequences of what is going on and the expected outcome from what you contemplate doing before acting—that's good advice. It is also evidence of good thinking.

"What can we expect will happen if certain actions are taken?" This is the question thinking people address practically every moment. Their eyes wide open, their minds fully engaged, these individuals don't just act safely, but also shrewdly. Many deadly accidents arise because people fail to consider the dangers involved in what they are doing. We all know that gasoline is highly flammable. We know what happens when gasoline ignites—and it takes only a tiny spark to ignite it. You would think that someone who handles gasoline tanks would know these things. Regardless, when a person's consciousness is disengaged, such knowledge is not going to protect him. A newspaper reported an incident in which a laborer was killed when a gasoline storage tank he was cutting with a portable power saw exploded. The worker's company was involved in installing, removing, and junking gasoline pumps and underground tanks. Although he had experience working with the saw and scrap metal the worker did not adequately purge the tank and test for vapors before beginning to cut. The 18 ft. × 6 ft., 3,000 gallon tank had been used recently for underground storage at a service station. At the time of the explosion the worker was cutting on the tank with a gasoline powered portable saw equipped with an abrasive epoxy disk for cutting metal. The explosion propelled the worker nearly fifteen feet from the tank into another tank.

Sometimes the explosions that harm us are not those that destroy our lives but the kind that can cripple our reputations and careers. We heard recently from a friend named Tom in San Francisco who works for a company that sells and installs office furniture. His company does not solicit client-customers directly but gets involved via referrals and invitations to make proposals through interior design firms. Tom told us about a salesman at a rival firm who all but destroyed his reputation. Instead of waiting for an invitation by an interior design firm to make a proposal, this salesperson went directly to their client company with a proposal. His actions infuriated the people at the interior design firm. As a result, the next time the people at the interior design firm seek out furniture suppliers, you can bet they will purposely leave this overly eager salesperson off their list of those they invite to make a proposal.

BE THE KIND OF PERSON OTHERS WANT TO BE AROUND

Value Feelings, Treat Others with Dignity, Be an Encourager

"One of life's supreme dangers is to value things more than people."

William Barclay

How we treat others matters. It matters more than anything else we do. It spells the difference between just being a person and being someone others want to know, work with, and have as a friend. In 1938, a gifted young fiddle player named Ervin T. Roush composed a piece of music that has electrified audiences ever since. His "Orange Blossom Special" is a favorite among fiddle enthusiasts because of its difficulties and rousing passages. But Roush was a troubled man; in his later years he played for tip money to buy drinks, and lived a reclusive life in a Florida backwoods shack that he built himself out of plywood. Fiddler Chubby Wise brought the song to national prominence. Although popular, it was Johnny Cash's creative rendition of "Orange Blossom Special" as a harmonica piece that really boosted its sales. Cash's recording added substantially to the stream of royalties going to composer Roush. Hattie Roush Miscowich, his widow, was most grateful to Johnny Cash for something she thought even more important, the ways in which he quietly assisted Ervin over the years. Ervin Roush was an alcoholic and suffered from mental illness, probably schizophrenia. He died in 1980, all but forgotten. But one person didn't forget. At Roush's sparsely attended memorial service a huge spray of flowers, orange in color and shaped like a train, was delivered to the funeral home. The sender was Johnny Cash. According to Hattie, Johnny Cash called during Ervin's final hospitalization and prayed with the old fiddler. She always remembered his compassion.

Some of life's struggles involve living with ourselves. We are given the capacity to know and understand our own nature and inclinations, our passions and tendencies. It is up to us, not someone else, to make ourselves into the persons we are capable of becoming. We need to learn how to use our minds effectively in thinking and choosing wisely. We need to learn how to direct our talents to good uses and develop them to their fullest. At the same time we are wise to respect the fact that we are not islands unto ourselves. We do not live and work apart from others, but with them. This, the other part of the human experience, involves developing the capacity to interact with others effectively. How can we do that?

The answer lies in being the kind of person that others want to be around. This does not mean trying to be just like others. That would not be authentic, nor would it be possible. But it does mean not being a nuisance. And it means acting in ways that uplift and enrich the lives of those with whom you interact day-to-day. Trying to make peace with the overly sensitive coworker who lives the part of the perpetual victim presents another set of problems altogether, which we will not go into here. We will consider, rather, how individuals can expand their capacity to treat others with respect, to be kind and caring, and to become as much concerned with their neighbor's well-being as they are with their own. Those who act in these ways make themselves much more human and their effectiveness in the workplace becomes greater because of it.

Eight Ways Not to Be a Pain in the Neck to Others

Problem people exist practically everywhere we go. They annoy and infuriate us. They cause trouble. They create problems that hold others back from performing their best at work. But this is not the worst of it: each one of us will be in their company at one time or another. Each one of us can be an unwanted nuisance at work, because we are human and have one or more of these tendencies. The best way to eliminate these pain-in-the-neck individuals from the workplace is to try to break our own inner tendencies to be a nuisance. Here are several commonly encountered nuisances.

Nuisance #1, The Complainer: Whether it's the color of freshly painted office walls or the new forklift truck in the warehouse, or an added benefit package, or safety inspections, the complainer will see something wrong with it. And it's usually a "wrong" that no one else sees or cares much about. Complainers are not happy unless they can be totally dissatisfied and show it. But they never stop there. They try to get others to share in what's making them so miserable. They want them to be miserable too! So, the complainer spends his time telling everyone who will stop and listen how poorly he is being treated, what the matter with this or that is, and why things are not good enough to suit him. We've heard his kind of complaints many times: His previous boss was so much better than his current boss. The company he used to work for was better than the one he works for now. The town he came from was superior to the one in which he now resides.

What we need to realize is that the complainer is driven by a desire to feel superior. We all want to feel that way, but we all are not so fixated on achieving that aim that we resort to destructive methods, as complainers do. Most smart people try to achieve distinction by doing things exceptionally well. The complainer is different because he is secretly aware of the fact that he does not have the ability to perform in superior ways. How then does he try to achieve distinction and make himself feel superior? He complains constantly. This all-knowing critic of the way things are makes it his business to articulate negatives, identify faults, and point out other people's failures. What he is really trying to tell us is, "I'm better than others."

Nuisance #2, The Constant Talker: Meetings that should take only twenty minutes stretch out over an hour. Greetings from people passing each other in the hallway end up consuming sometimes five to ten minutes. And telephone calls for specific pieces of information can turn into irritating drains on one's nerves. All these kinds of things happen because of the constant talker, the person who cannot seem to keep her mouth shut. While most normal people crave human contact, and some of us need and enjoy more of it than others, there is a difference between the person who talks enough and the person who simply talks too much. There are many reasons for the highly talkative type of personality. Most constant talkers just have a high need for affiliation. They seek out others for companionship, to be energized from interpersonal relationships. But there are other types of constant talkers who have a different agenda—these types want to impress us with what they know, with their gossip, with their inside scoops on the latest happenings, with their technical know-how. Another reason why some people talk too much is that they have not made up their mind about an issue or don't quite know what they should think or feel about something that's just come up. Rather than quietly pondering the matter, they think it through verbally, talking their way through it, and demonstrating to all within hearing range how confused and uncertain of themselves they are. Their thinking processes are completely scrambled. Constant talkers search for willing listeners. Frequently, they stick their noses into places where they don't belong. They butt into other people's conversations, inserting their own opinions and stories uninvited. They are also the first to circulate the latest rumors; gossip is their business and they seem to take pride in the fact that they are not just the first to know something but, most importantly, the first to get the word out to others.

I (Charles) recall once hearing one of these types prattle on about aircraft design during a dinner-table conversation. The person voicing his scientific opinions seemed to think he knew all there was to know about aircraft design, even though he had never studied the subject or designed even a tiny part of an aircraft himself. Quietly seated at the same dinner table and saying nothing sat a highly paid aeronautical engineer who rolled his eyes as the constant talker, wanting attention, pontificated.

Nuisance #3, The Bragger: A mother brags about her seventh grade son who got all A's on his last report card. A father boasts of his daughter's three first-place finishes at her high school's swim meet. A truck driver tells others how he shaves time off delivery route schedules. These are the lines coming from the mouths of braggers, persons we would just as soon avoid because a little of their self-flattery goes more than a long way, it goes past our level of tolerance. The bragger wants others to think he is wonderful largely because he isn't fully convinced of it himself. If he can get others to nod in agreement that what he did or what his child has accomplished was wonderful, then he's assured that what he did was exceptional. To boost his self-assurance, he will tell of whatever it is that he owns—a new car, a piece of property, a special piece of equipment—that he feels will impress others. If he has money in the bank or a well-paid job, it's certain that he will bring up these ego-satisfying facts.

What's worth understanding about the bragger is that she is actually dependent on the approval of others. She isn't comfortable with her own judgments and thinks she needs something more than the satisfaction that simply comes from accomplishing things. There is a curious phenomenon at work behind braggers and it is this: Success itself is never enough to satisfy them. They are their own worst enemy because they want something more than success itself. They want praise and lots of it. Tragically, praise is something that is never fully satisfying. These people are their own worst enemy because they are driven not to accomplish things but to receive praise for their accomplishments. They accomplish something that deserves praise and they receive it. But the praise is never enough. They want still more praise and to get it they resort to bragging, expecting the praise to keep flowing their way.

Nuisance #4, The One-Upper: Imagine the scene—someone has turned in a superior performance and congratulatory praises are being showered on the person deserving recognition. Perhaps this person has just landed a huge order from a much sought-after customer, or maybe she has solved a logjam on a production line, or maybe she came up with a money-saving method that improved product quality. Whatever it was that the hero of the moment did, it deserves recognition and almost everyone is glad to say, "Well done." Everyone, that is, but the dazzler, the "one-upper," the person who wants so much to be noticed and appreciated and paid attention to that she will try to impress others with her accomplishment of a similar nature. Whenever praise is flowing toward someone else, these types try to snag some of it for themselves, so hungry are they for attention and recognition.

One observer characterized this type as a person who can always outdo your story because he (or she) has a vast life experience and needs to talk about it to anyone who will listen. According to the one-uppers of the world, they have done everything there is to do in the world and they have done these things better than anyone else ever has or ever will.

Nuisance #5, The Beater-Downer: In formal meetings or casual discussions between a few coworkers there can sometimes be found the annoying person who makes a nuisance of himself by trying to beat down other people's ideas. Instead of seeing the good points in what other people have to say, the beater-downer finds it appropriate—and secretly amusing—to point out in no uncertain terms where they are dead wrong. But the beater-downer does not merely find fault with ideas and suggestions posed by others. The beater-downer goes much further and attacks others personally. In their minds they "win" by putting others down. They appear to take joy in the humiliation of others. The motive behind this nuisance is not so much the honest critical analysis of ideas and suggestions as it is the desire to show how much smarter and better they are themselves. And they do this by trying to make others appear dumb, naïve, misinformed. What's so annoying about these people is that there is just enough truth in what they say for those who are honest in their thinking to recognize the flaws in any idea posed. The beater-downers in our world take advantage of the fact that every idea or suggestion, whatever it might be, has some negative aspect, flaw, or shortcoming. This is because we live in an imperfect world in which there is no flawless answer to any problem or to any situation requiring a response. Beater-downers of the world argue for the sake of arguing; it's their most developed quality and they use it for all it's worth.

Nuisance #6, The Work-Escaper: The work-escapers fear being thought of as less capable and less competent than others. This is one reason why they will do everything possible to avoid work—they fear criticism for making mistakes or for doing things differently than those who might criticize them. It is common for work-escapers to delay beginning a job. They frequently bring up the reasonable-sounding excuse that "We need to know more about the situation and what's expected of us before we begin." Fear of failure and the possibility of ridicule that might follow dominate the work-escaper's fears. Their fears are more substantial than others might imagine. Fear can choke off the desire to take a first step. Fears can paralyze a person from trying. If severe pressure is placed on them to do something and procrastination is no longer possible, they try to find someone else to do their work for them. Moreover, they are good at doing this, knowing just how to pull the right levers to goad, flatter, or entice others into doing what they ought to be doing themselves.

Work-escapers frequently turn to superiors for help. They demand to be told how to perform the tiniest details, so unwilling are they to think for themselves. Over time their fears and dependence on others lead them down the path of ineffectiveness and they stall out. They accomplish very little. Finally, their pattern of leaning on others becomes so widely known and understood that their willing dupes turn on them and let them "hang out to dry."

Nuisance #7, The "I'm Special" Person: One of the most destructive and annoying nuisances is the person whose sole concern is self. Their entire world is encapsulated within the boundaries of the little two-letter word, *me*. After being around them for any amount of time others will say of them, "It's all about 'ME,' isn't it?" It is not just a little word but it is also a little matter, the self. Whatever the issue is, whether it is a revised vacation schedule, a new work procedure, or a change in policies, the "I'm special" person looks at it through the lens of self—"How will it affect me?" they ask. Forget about the benefits that may come to customers, or to others in the work group, or to those who depend on the organization performing effectively and being competitive. The "I'm special" person is not the least bit interested in anything beyond self and how changes will disrupt his quietude, his status, his workload, his comfortable routine.

We see the "I'm special" person in action most clearly when standards, procedures, or rules are in place. The "I'm special" person does not object to these things, they merely object to the idea that standards, procedures, and rules should apply to everyone equally. As they see it, they are "more equal" than others. They act as if they are above the guidelines everyone else is expected to follow. They place themselves first and see only their wants and needs. And so, when two women work in an office and each wants to take a vacation day on the same Friday but work demands that at least one be there, a conflict arises. One of the two will have to forego her wishes and come in to work. Jeanne wants to use the day to stay home and clean her house and make preparations for her daughter's first communion and family gathering afterward on Sunday. Connie wants the day off to go shopping with a friend, and since she has more seniority, she gets her wish. She could have seen things in a larger perspective but she didn't. She could have been concerned about the other person, but she wasn't.

Nuisance #8, The Credit-Grabber: Credit-grabbers act the part of thieves. Some will do it secretly, behind our backs. Others are not so subtle; they steal credit for themselves overtly, shamelessly. The first job our friend Gail took right out of college was a clerk position in the personnel office of a building supply company. She had been on the job just a few weeks when Neil, the Human Resources director, came to her with a special project. He asked Gail to develop a job bidding procedure for the company. When a new position opened up that paid more than the existing starting pay grade, management felt that those who were already employed by the company should have first chance to apply for these better-paying jobs. Now it became Gail's responsibility to research the idea and establish the policies and procedures for job bidding. Working with supervisors in the plant, Gail learned the practical difficulties of carrying out a job bidding procedure. It wasn't as simple as she first imagined it would be but she stuck with it and over several weeks' time, she developed a set of policies and procedures that supervisors endorsed. Once she had her program laid out in writing, Gail composed a cover memo introducing the new procedures. This would be sent with the new procedures to all departments throughout the company. Gail showed her completed work to Neil, her boss. He studied it over carefully and said, "Gail, this is wonderful. I want you to introduce this tomorrow." And with that he picked up the memo that Gail had prepared, crossed out her name and wrote his in its place. "Retype this," he told her.

Learn to See the Human Dimensions

Many years ago, when I (Charles) worked for Anaconda Copper I spent a morning with the manager of the maintenance department at our company's mine south of Tucson, Arizona. Here workers repaired heavy earthmoving equipment: haulers, scrapers, belly-loaders, and the like. Workmen busily went about their tasks, tearing apart the broken machinery, locating the problems, getting the right tools and equipment, putting the equipment back together. As the maintenance manager and I walked down the center aisle of the large steel building where repairs were performed, he enthusiastically explained his department's function. He told of its difficulties—the problems he had finding and training competent mechanics and technicians. As we walked along, I noticed that the men working there seemed to be avoiding this manager. The workmen appeared to dart out of his way so as to avoid eye contact with him. All the while, this manager continued to explain to me how his operation ran. Suddenly, the manager stopped dead in his tracks. Apparently he spotted something that was terribly important to him. He paused and watched for a moment and then walked directly to where a man was working on an earthmover. Coming up from behind the man, the manager nudged the workman out of the way. I surmised that the manager had spotted something that the workman was doing wrong. I gauged the event correctly. The manager told the workman that the problem with the broken machine was much larger and more serious than the minor difficulty he was fixing. He explained what needed to be done and the workman nodded in agreement.

What I noticed that morning and what the maintenance manager noticed in the workplace were entirely different things. I noticed things emotional. The maintenance manager noticed things mechanical. Where the maintenance manager saw broken equipment, the time being spent repairing it, and the time being wasted doing things wrong, I noticed the ways workmen avoided this man and how the one he brushed aside appeared embarrassed over the incident. The point is that humans see what they want to see. They are sensitive to what they value and understand. The significance of this fact is that in any work situation there is to be found a host of matters that run the gamut from financial to mechanical and from human to technological. It is difficult, perhaps impossible, for one person to see the many elements that exist. Some people see only a narrow few, and these are usually what they are either trained to see or ones which nature and temperament incline them to see. Part of our world consists of things tangible, things that we can see, touch, measure. Another part of our world consists of things intangible, things that we can sense, feel, experience with our emotions. Logical and emotional—these are the two halves of the human experience. Each one is vitally important. Our very existence involves both dimensions. But it is the realm of the emotional—the feelings people experience—that most affects relationships.

As a young man I (Tom) worked summers repairing railroad tracks in the west. The work was dirty, difficult, and tiring. It required physical stamina, especially during the hottest months of the summer when July and August sun beat down across the desert-like terrain and temperatures touched the 100-degree mark. As a member of a work crew, a man is required to show effort, to hold up his end, not to "wimp out." Work has to be done right; no shortcuts are permitted because the consequences of a single mistake can be enormous. The chance of a freight train or a passenger train going off the tracks if they are ill-aligned or rough is not slight. So when tracks wear down from years of use and nature's elements work to decay and shift roadbeds, work crews must make repairs—removing the old and worn and replacing them with new sections of rails. This involves digging up roadbeds, tearing out worn or twisted rails, replacing heavy, creosote-soaked ties, setting new tracks into the correct position. Driving spikes, moving tons of gravel, lifting and setting steel rails—these are the duties of a work crew. But these things must not be done carelessly. Tracks must be aligned exactly, the grade and pitch and turns have to be set accurately if trains are to run smoothly and safely across the landscape.

One might think that under such conditions—the heat, the heavy lifting, the dirt, the difficulty of getting things right under inhospitable conditions—crew members would hate their work. One might also think that morale would be rock-bottom low under these difficult conditions. It was just the opposite. With common obstacles and the need to work together if anything were to get done, work crews took pride in the fact that they could accomplish the difficult under back-breaking conditions. We defeated the boredom and beat back the sun's relentless rays by talking to each other. We told stories, exchanged jokes, poked fun at each other, did things we would not do back on the streets of the towns we came from. Our work was tough but we were tougher. We were friends, not competitors; we had to be. The camaraderie we shared kept us coming back each day for more work. We were able to work more effectively, more productively, and more happily because we knew each other and we shared a common pur-pose and fought against a common set of difficulties. Each day, at quitting time, we parted with a sense that we would return to work the next morning not to boring, dirty, difficult work, but to friends. What drew us back each day was the good humor, the feeling of being part of something larger than ourselves—it was something we counted on, just as we counted on the cooperation we gave in getting our jobs done right.

How people feel about themselves, about their work, and about each other in the workplace spells the difference between high-level performance and satisfaction and dreadful results—low-quality output and strained relationships. The emotional, not the observable forces that we can see directly and measure, matter most in determining whether work is pleasant or painful. The physical realities, the bottom-line measures, the things tangible and obvious—these are what anyone can see and what most people pay attention to. Yet is our neglect of things emotional—attitudes, feelings, hopes and fears, all the consid-erations we cannot touch and put into clear measurable terms—that most often leads to failure. Here is a simple illustration of this point.

Many years ago, top management of an expanding oil company decided money could be saved and bottom-line results improved if they moved the sales staff located in downtown offices to vacant space at a refinery on the outskirts of town. Despite the substantial cost savings to the company that came from the move, employees complained about it bitterly. The refinery location was noisy and dirty, but that wasn't what bothered them most. It was that they felt shoved aside. Their opinions were not considered; and they were not involved in the decision. Employees knew that the company was doing well financially, so, why were expenses being slashed? Top management ignored the complaints. They told the employees, "Get used to it." Soon the employees began to think differently about those in charge. Their liking of upper management turned into disliking. The positive attitudes and high morale that came from feeling they were part of a "winning" organization soured. They began looking for things that were "wrong" and their negative attitudes opened their eyes to many possibilities. Some employees began saying openly that "the company was going to the dogs." And here we come face to face with an important question: Despite record-high sales and earnings, was the company "going to the dogs?"

The answer one gives to this question reveals whether he or she sees and values the vital importance of things unseen, emotions and feelings. Do attitudes and morale and feelings really matter all that much? If people feel that their organization is "going to the dogs" will that feeling eventually play itself out in actuality? Will these negative feelings and attitudes cause the enterprise real and lasting harm? Most people prefer to be around those who are logical and sensitive, those who have a good sense of proportion, and those who realize the value of things logical and emotional. The husband who dismisses his wife's hurt feelings and anger after she lets him know how she feels about his forgetting her birthday is setting himself up for a very unhappy home life. What woman in her right mind feels safe and loved when the man she is married to ignores her, paying more attention to other things that are "more important" to him? A helpful idea to keep in mind is that emotions matter. People "live" where their hearts are and their hearts—if they are healthy and normal—are usually consumed by emotions, feelings, not with things rational and tangible.

Value the Emotional Dimensions in Interactions

From a recent experience I (Charles) have become more aware than ever of the importance of valuing the emotional dimensions in every situation. It is generally a good idea to view every interaction we have with others as emotional encounters, where feelings are present and run deep. All too often, people "step on others," so to speak. They might not mean to do it but, nonetheless, that's exactly what they do. A perfect illustration of this occurred when I was one of a group of volunteers building a playground at a local park. Men, women, and kids had volunteered their time through various business and service organizations to construct a play site for their community. One evening while I stood at my post, handing out tools and supplies as needed, a man approached me and asked what was going on. This man had come to the park that evening and found the place alive with building activity. I told him about the project. The man was struck by the spirit of involvement of those who had volunteered. The idea of giving one's talents intrigued him. He had skills that he could offer to the project and he wanted to make them available. He told me that he was a heavy-equipment operator, with considerable work experience. "Who do I see?" he asked. I pointed to one of the project leaders and the man went over to speak to him. A few minutes later, the man came back my way, his head low. The buoyant enthusiasm he had when we parted minutes earlier had evaporated. The man appeared dejected. "What did you find out?" I asked him. "They don't have any use for me," he said.

It struck me as terribly inconsiderate of the project leader to send this potential contributor and helper away in this manner. Instead of making a friend and supporter, he created a potential enemy. At the very least he made a human being feel bad. While it may have been true that the project did not need a heavy-equipment operator, it was also obviously true that it could still use another person with construction skills and know-how. Maybe this man had other talents and interests that could be used. By treating the situation in a purely logical way, seeing only the obvious facts of the situation, the project leader missed the emotional side, a side that probably mattered more both to the project itself and to whether those working on it would come to respect or despise the leader.

Never Try to Force Others to Feel the Way You Think They Should Feel

In every shop and office across the country there are plenty of things about which people will readily disagree. A new piece of equipment is installed to help boost productivity: some people will feel threatened while others will welcome it. A change in hiring procedures is ordered by top management: some people will view it as a blessing, others as a curse. A new person joins a work group: some of the coworkers will be supportive while others will be negative. It is always helpful to remember that along with tangible, observable conditions and events, there will also be personal responses, emotional reactions. Many times people will differ in how they feel about things. Some will be positive, others negative. Consider the situation when a new employee is hired. One of the coworkers might like this new person who, to her, appears friendly. "The new woman in our department is going to make a big difference. She's got such terrific enthusiasm and her experience is impressive. She's so friendly," the first coworker says. Another coworker reacts differently, saying, "I don't know. I think she's rather pushy; a real troublemaker, if you ask me. Besides, I heard that she had to leave her last job because they couldn't stand her."

Whenever people find that their opinions and feelings about something differ from those of others, something curious occurs. Rather than simply accepting the fact that another person sees or feels differently there is always a tendency to try to change that other person's opinions and feelings to comport with one's own. This tendency is frequently the source of disputes and rarely works as it is intended, to change the other person's mind. In fact, it generally hardens their position.

Getting along with others requires respecting them as persons, with minds and emotions of their own. One of the most annoying things a person can do is to try to manipulate or dictate what another person should feel about something. Whether that something is a change in a work schedule, the actions of a coworker, a newly installed computer system, or whatever, everyone will have some type of emotional reaction to it. Everyone will experience something very real and very important: an inner feeling, be it a fear, joy, or worry. We do not choose how we feel. While it is true that we can choose how we behave in the face of events—self-control enables us to hold back from acting on our anger from time to time—it is also true that we do not choose to make ourselves feel as we do. Feelings just happen and there we are, left to deal with them as we choose. It also bears mentioning that the feelings we have are our own, personal reactions. We have ours just as others have theirs.

Telling someone how we feel about something is one thing. Telling another person how he or she ought to feel about it is another matter entirely. Trying to force another person to feel the way you do about something inevitably invites conflict. Here is why. As individuals with minds and feelings of our own, our sense of individuality is threatened when someone tries to tell us how we should feel. It is as though the person trying to tell us how to feel is saying that our true feelings are of no importance and only those of this other person are. Likewise, we hate it when others try to convince us that we ought to feel about something the same way they feel about it. We resent the person who tries to dominate us and argue us out of what we think and feel. We value our freedom to have preferences, and we naturally resent anyone who tries to take away our freedom to be a fully independent human with likes and dislikes of our own. We resist them because their conflicting opinions and feelings threaten our sense of reality. Still, we all have a tendency to make this same mistake.

You have probably noticed a phenomenon that occurs whenever a speaker or performer says or does something that evokes a strong reaction. At these moments many people will turn to the person seated next to them—usually the person they came with—and check their reaction, as if to confirm that they had the same response as they did. Humans seem to feel better when those close to them feel the same way about things as they do. It is reassuring. They seem to connect in a way so as to relive the moment just enjoyed, the joke, the enjoyable surprise just witnessed. Most likely people tend to do this because there is something deep within their human nature that craves for approval and security. We tend to want verification that our feelings are justified and right and sensible. Perhaps this explains why, whenever we react to something, we immediately seek out others to check their reaction against ours. It makes us feel secure when we know that we are not out of touch with reality and are safely within the bounds of good judgment. But what does one do when the other person has an entirely different reaction? Imagine two people seated next to each other in a meeting in which upper management announces that one of a group's coworkers will assume the duties of supervisor. This person has worked alongside the others and has both pleased and offended various members of the group. One person says to another, "I think this is a good decision. I like it." Another person, hearing this comment, responds, "This decision will turn out to be a disaster. They picked the wrong person." An argument ensues that involves each person restating her opinion, each time more strongly than the time before. As they try to convince each other of what they believe to be the correct opinion, they also challenge the other person's right to hold the feelings and opinions that they do.

Think of it: We hear someone make a controversial remark or do something we strongly like or dislike. What is our immediate reaction? It is to either agree or disagree with what the person said or did and then try to get others nearby to agree with our point of view. But we don't let it go at that. We are not happy unless everyone around us agrees with the way we see things, and feels the same way as we feel about them. And when we learn that others do not, our immediate reaction is to try to make them think and feel the way we do by arguing them out of their obviously wrongheaded positions. But this is never as straightforward and simple as we imagine it will be. Although we try to get others to go along with our way of thinking, they inevitably resist. And it seems that the harder we try the harder they resist. What is occurring here is much like what happens when you walk outside on a cold winter day, the wind screaming past. The harder the wind blows against you, the more tightly you pull your coat around yourself.

Trying to argue another person out of his point of view and feelings is counterproductive. Telling him he has no right to feel the way he does causes him to dig in his heels all the deeper, holding his ground. The best way to change another person's deep-seated opinions or feelings about an important matter is to simply understand that other person and let that person know that you do. Trying to use logic and reason to alter another person's deeply held views and feelings is futile. A human will change only when that person chooses to change and the choice to change never arrives when icy winds of disagreement are blowing in their direction, causing them to hold all the more tightly to their convictions. Whenever a person tries to tell another how he or she ought to feel, that person is also saying more than the obvious. The manipulator is also saying that the other person's perceptions, judgments, and logic are all wrong. Who wants to hear that?

Treat Other People's Self-Image Respectfully

A man we know named Mike has been a carpenter all his life. His father and his uncle were both carpenters. And their father, Mike's grandfather, was a carpenter too. Mike took great pride in telling others that his grandfather was one of the first carpenters in the area to use an electric skill saw. As far back as he could remember and while going out to job sites where his dad worked, Mike knew in his heart that he wanted some day to build homes. And, as soon as he graduated from high school, he began working for his father full-time. Now in his mid-forties, Mike works on his own. In the course of twenty-five years he has accumulated many experiences and solved practically every kind of building challenge imaginable. He is experienced and competent, confident in his knowledge and abilities.

Jobs used to come to Mike regularly but the seasonal nature of the building and the boom and bust periods of construction sometimes bring days or weeks of idleness, with little home-building going on. During one of these turndowns in building activity Mike hired out to work on a large project, the building of a strip mall. Here he was not alone in charge of the job, as he was accustomed to being in the building of individual homes. Instead, on this project, he worked under the general direction of a construction supervisor. The supervisor was a twenty-seven-year-old engineer who had risen rapidly in the ranks of a growing construction company.

One morning during his first week working on the project Mike spotted what he considered a minor mistake in the plans. He'd read plans practically all his life and he knew that finding minor errors in them is not unusual. If one understands basic construction methods and how things are put together, errors in plans are easily spotted and the correct steps are obvious. Mike proceeded with what he knew to be the conventional way of framing the part of the building he was constructing. Mike's supervisor, a man named Jack, came by where Mike was working and looked at the plan. He noticed that Mike was doing something different and called him on it.

"That isn't what the plan calls for," Jack said. "Can't you read simple blueprints?"

"Yes. I can read prints," said Mike. "I've been reading them long before you were able to walk."

"Look, you," said Jack in a scolding tone. "On this job we do what the plan calls for, not what you feel like doing. I thought you said that you knew how to build; you bragged about all your experience when you came for this job. I don't think you know as much as you think you do."

Mike felt his temper beginning to flare up. "You might have a college degree, but you don't know as much about framing as you think you do. All you know is what comes out of books. Let me tell you something, Sonny. If I built the thing here exactly the way these plans call for, you'd end up failing an inspection and have to rebuild this section. Do you want to lose a week or more re-doing work that wasn't done right in the first place? Besides, what do you know? None of your books could solve all the problems I've solved in my years of experience. You're too dumb to spot a simple mistake in these plans; that's something your books never taught you."

As the conflict escalated, tempers flared. Mike said things that offended Jack's opinion of himself and Jack returned these "insults" to Mike, in kind. And the more one person said to the other person, the more demeaning, the more threatening the comments became. It would not be too long, were this conflict to continue, before the two would be at each other's throats, likely exchanging punches. Each man believes he is competent. Each sees himself as capable. Yet, in this situation, each man says things that challenge the other's self-image. Here, in epitome, is the nature of interpersonal conflict. As each man mocks the other's self-image, each becomes more defensive, more hostile, and more aggressive. And, as the cycle continues, the situation becomes even more heated, the adversaries even more hostile and unreasonable. Calm and sensible dialog and mutual understanding become less possible.

If you want to put another person on the defensive, making that person an instant enemy, here's the formula: Verbally attack that person's self-image. This will usually cause the other person to return fire, attacking your self-image. From here on it's attack and counterattack, each time with increased intensity.

Share the Sandbox

One important feature of today's workplace is that most people do not work independently, but with others. The days of the cobbler working alone proudly repairing shoes by himself, needing no one, have passed. Today, work is performed in teams. If we are to be successful in today's workplaces, we must learn to become productive team members—each one of us needs to contribute our share and cooperate with others. In the modern corporation today, knowing how to cooperate and share responsibilities and value the ideas and talents and efforts of others is essential.

How good are we at working alongside others? Just the other day, while walking through a nearby park, we noticed children playing in a sandbox. How happy they seemed filling their buckets with sand and moving it from one spot to another. The mood of fun and the laughter changed suddenly when a larger child stepped into the sandbox and began shouting out orders: "Give me that. Don't do it that way. Make the pile over here." The others there ignored the intruder. But that did not deter the bully from attempting to take control of what went on. How similar this child's play experience is to what goes on in meetings, in small groups, and in entire divisions of modern-day organizations. There is ample evidence to suggest that some adults have difficulty moving beyond the childish ways they used to get their way when they were very young. Not long ago at their monthly meeting the board of trustees of a local church discussed a problem of how to provide wheelchair access to the church's meeting hall. One possibility involved building a ramp. Another method was to install a mechanical lift. And the last idea was to bring in fill material and regrade the side yard, making it higher, so that a new sidewalk could be built right up to the entrance.

One of the trustees, a man named Tim, had considered all three ideas and had already come to the conclusion that the mechanical lift was the best solution. Others on the board were not so sure. The other possible solutions seemed better to them but they wanted to discuss all three to be sure. Tim announced his preference at the outset of the meeting and defended it with an air of superiority: "The lift is by far the best way to provide wheelchair access. The other approaches are too costly and present either aesthetic or water problems to the building." Another member of the board, a woman named June, thought the regrading of the ground on the side of the building sounded like a better idea. When she brought up this possibility, Tim shot back, "You don't know a thing about how water problems are caused do you, June? If you build up the side yard, there's no place for the water to escape. It will seep into the side of the building. Just go out and look at how the ground around the building slopes. Can't you see it?" June sank back in her chair. Tim felt puffed up by his superior knowledge and he believed that the other trustees were impressed by his strong stand. Next, Rod suggested the ramp idea, which caused Tim to strike out like a cobra. "That's going to look terrible, running all the way out to the street. Besides, you haven't a clue as to how much something like that will cost."

It doesn't take a genius to spot the person who is unable to "share the sandbox." They act in ways to make themselves appear strong, decisive, powerful—persons others dare not challenge or question. They feel that they have superior knowledge and experience, and that their ideas and methods are above criticism. Whenever other points of view are offered or other methods attempted, the person who insists on taking charge and calling all the shots reacts with belittling sarcasm. To the person unwilling to share the sandbox, ideas from others are a threat to the status and power they crave. Whenever different ideas are suggested this person "puts them down."

Learn to Lift Others Up

One of the most remarkable qualities you can develop is the ability to inspire others to better possibilities. This involves far more than glad-handing and saying nice things to others, trying to make them feel good. Instead, it involves doing or saying the right kinds of things that will awaken something deep within their souls to want to do new and exciting things. With just the right words of genuine concern and encouragement, you can help others to blossom out and grow into better persons and performers. Lifting up others involves both emotional and intellectual powers; and it is an ability that separates great leaders from those who think they are leaders. It is not difficult to spot whether a person possesses such a quality, the ability to uplift and inspire, by what they say and do to others. We become acutely aware of the opposite in people any time discouragement and negativity appear. A woman we know, named Holly, has worked in the fields of public information and publicity all her professional career. She is highly educated and experienced in writing and making news releases for organizations. Holly is regarded as a highly competent professional at the University where she has been employed for many years. A delicate situation arose once. It needed the skills of an experienced newsperson in how best to release critical information to the public. Holly offered a thoughtful suggestion. The University's president, Jim, didn't like having an underling offer a suggestion, especially a suggestion that was unsolicited. He told Holly, "You are a doer around here, not a thinker." The sharp comment not only stunned Holly, but it further alienated the president from those who worked under him—and the story spread throughout the community, further alienating him from the rank and file.

We do ourselves a great service and help others enormously at the same time whenever we are encouraging and helpful. Here is a simple illustration of what we mean. Ten years ago, and after her daughter was full grown and on her own, a woman we met named Jane Farris returned to college where she completed the last three years work she needed for a degree. Jane had an aptitude for numbers and details and was interested in legal issues. These interests led her to specialize in compensation management, which is part of the human resources function. She had worked for a medium-sized high-tech company seven years when her boss left for another position. Naturally, Jane felt that she was the person best prepared to fill her boss's shoes and she went to the VP of human resources, Hiram Jackson, to tell him of her interest in the vacant position. Although a bit apprehensive about talking so bluntly about her credentials and her sincere interest in the position, Jane was determined to make her case to higher-ups.

"I'm glad you agreed to see me, Mr. Jackson," she said. "I've wanted to talk to you about my work and the position that has just opened up."

Jackson shuffled papers on his desk as Jane spoke. When she finished he gazed across the room as if he were in deep thought. "You know," he said, "I'm beginning to think that a lot of people are expecting to be selected for this important job. What makes you think you have the experience and knowledge it requires?"

Jane didn't know how to respond. Jackson's words and tone made her feel uncomfortable. Jane felt that she was imposing on his time and that he didn't want her to be in his office with him at all. She wanted to get up and walk out but she knew that she was the one who had approached the VP and now she had to follow through with what she wanted to say. "I've been in this department for seven years now and we've gone through a lot of growth. There have been many changes and I have been at the center of them. I think I can continue making important changes in the future too. I have experience," she said.

"You and a lot of other people have experience too, Jane," he said. "How familiar are you with the new legislation being proposed? We need someone who knows their stuff. We cannot afford to run afoul of the law. Another thing, how well do you think you can sell our new procedures to those in the field? You seem to have spent all your time here in the office and we are going to need a person who can get out and convince operating managers to follow the procedures we've set up. What makes you think you can do that? I don't see you as someone with those skills. You have a reputation for doing so-so work, sitting at a desk behind a computer, and reading up on the law. I haven't seen anything that would give me confidence in your ability to get others to go along with what we need to implement."

Wrapped up with one's own role and sense of power and importance, it is not difficult to forget about the other person's feelings. So intent can one be to show his or her superiority and power, that the chance to uplift and inspire others is missed. In the interchange between Hiram Jackson and Jane Ferris we first see that Jackson ignored Jane. He was busy with things that he found more important. What do you think that said to Jane? Next, he put her on the defensive—not exactly the best way to open up lines of communication and invite deeply held aspirations and ambitions to be voiced. Lastly, he challenged Jane's basic competence, making her feel that he thinks she is incapable of doing anything more difficult and challenging than she does now.

How differently Jane might have come away from that meeting had Jackson been authentically interested in and supportive of her. Let's consider what a person in Jackson's position could have done in this situation to encourage Jane? To begin with, the listener should have put everything aside and paid strict attention to Jane, giving her his full attention. This would say to her, *I think you are important and I think what you want to talk about is important.* This simple action alone will open up communication lines. Putting Jane at ease will encourage her to say things she might not feel safe in saying otherwise. Bear in mind, the smartest thing Jackson can do is to find out all he can about Jane because that will help him make a better-informed decision about filling the vacant position.

Next, Jackson should have welcomed Jane: "Jane, I'm glad you came to talk about this job you are interested in. Tell me something more about yourself and what changes you have in mind for the department." As she responds, Jackson would do well to listen intently and smile approvingly. Make the atmosphere warm and sunny—that's the smartest way to stimulate ideas and the free flow of information as someone opens up to you. Jackson ought not to challenge or argue with Jane as she speaks. Instead he would do better to pick out the parts of what she says that interest him and that he approves of and get her to talk more about those ideas. Remember, the purpose Jackson ought to hold in mind is to hear what Jane has to say, not to get into an argument with her and not to make her feel small because he might not think she is the best person for the job. The idea is to get Jane to feel comfortable and speak about herself, her ideas, and how she feels about the organization. By treating someone respectfully and encouragingly, Jackson will learn far more than he would by acting otherwise. And, when Jane walks out of his office, she will feel she has been treated nicely, as every human being ought to be treated. He hasn't promised her the job by treating her well and by acting in an encouraging way. If he selects someone else, Jane will always feel that at least she was respected by her boss.

BREAK THE CHAINS OF MINDLESS ROUTINE

Exercise Your Imagination, Turn Failures and Mistakes into Lessons, Rise Above Mediocrity

"Routines are ever present, and it is far easier to accept current practices than to question prevailing views or experiment with untried approaches."

David A. Garvin

We asked a production supervisor named Don recently, "What improvements have you made in the ways you do things at work lately?" He immediately wanted to set us straight about the pressures working people face every day that get in the way of their creative impulses. It was clear that Don thought we were naïve idealists and clueless as to why busy people rarely use their imaginations. Our question launched him into an explanation of how he saw things:

"In my line of work you have to stay focused on finishing the job at hand. We're under lots of pressure here to get things done on time. I have deadlines to meet. We also have quality standards that must be met and the only way to make sure that happens is to go by the book. I'd like to try out other methods but they might not work out or they might take too long to implement, and then where would I be? If you try out something new and it fails, you're in for a lot of criticism. You'd never live it down.

"I've thought of ways to improve how we do things now and then. This morning, for instance, I had an idea for a faster way of laying out work. But I quickly put it out of my mind because of the time pressures we're under. Besides it would probably be too complicated to explain to others. So, I scrapped the idea. I guess everyone thinks of new and better ways of doing their work from time to time. But you cannot go around changing things every other day. If you tried that, nothing would ever get done. No, I don't think it's a good idea to try some fancy, untested method. Besides, I think it is safer to stay with what you know works. It's just safer that way."

Break Free of Entrenched Ways and Mindless Routine

One of Don's admirable qualities is that he's practical; but, maybe he's too practical. In his drive to get work done quickly and correctly he never deviates from established methods. The result is that Don gets his work done on time, and it is always done right. These are good qualities. Yet something deep within Don is not right. He's dissatisfied with his work. He's dissatisfied with himself, and he's dissatisfied with his prospects for an exciting future. We see a good bit of cynicism coming out of Don. We believe Don secretly feels that he isn't the fully alive person he could be—and he's right. He isn't! But he's not alone. Look around and you'll see millions of others in the world who are just like Don—people who work hard but at the end of the day find themselves unfulfilled. Their minds are trapped by set ways of seeing things and doing things. They strive for safety and security above all else. Hidden deep within the hearts of these people, we see a debilitating worry: "What if I fail and others criticize me?" Under time pressures to get work out and pestered by worries about failure and the embarrassment that might follow, many able men and women resign themselves to doing things in the same old ways, following tried and true paths. All the while they try to silence the voice coming from their imaginations. They say to themselves, "Better not to think. Just do." Yet, all the while they feel something is missing—excitement in their work.

A pathetic aspect of life today is the astounding numbers of able-bodied men and women who are flat, dull, frozen, bored, cynical. Their minds appear to be asleep, their zest for living extinguished. While their plight may not be entirely of their own choosing, it is, nonetheless, partly of their own making. Unknowingly and unintentionally they are allowing themselves to grow stale, tired, bored, unhappy. Despite the many promptings and challenges coming their way that might excite their imaginations, they continue doing things in the same old ways. Instead of seeing and implementing new methods, instead of discovering new truths and possibilities, and instead of creating improvements and implementing them, they conform to past practices. They follow unchanging routines. Over time their powers of imagination will weaken, their enthusiasm for working will grow dull. It cannot be denied that we work under tension. Pulling us in one direction is our desire to be alive human beings using our imaginations, our powers of seeing possibilities for improvement. Yet, at the same time other forces tug at us to perform. There are deadlines, time clocks, and established standards that must be met.

The circumstances that lead to mindless routine are widely understood. A piece of work must be done now; a problem has to be solved right away; an opportunity must be pounced on immediately. Management gives the assignment to someone. It has a deadline. Little is done at first because the person is uncertain as to how to proceed. She fears making a mistake. Tension builds. Shortly, other fears take root and she secretly worries to herself, "What will others think if I try a different method and it fails?" She wonders what to do, how to proceed so as to hold on to her self-esteem. These worries dominate her thinking. She tries to figure out a foolproof method but realizes untested novelty is too risky. In the end she says to herself, "I will find what someone else did that worked in a similar situation and do that. I will copy what they did. It will probably work out okay. If it doesn't, I will have an excuse."

Maybe the most distressing aspects of unthinking routine is what it does to an individual's sense of self and their future possibilities with each passing year. When you peel away their cynicism and the layers of face-saving excuses they give for remaining mired in worn-out practices and not using their imaginations, you discover something very disturbing—how they feel about themselves: "It's too late for me to be imaginative." "I can't keep up with all this change going on around me." "I don't want to be wrong and look foolish. So, I will stick with what I know." "I don't have the luxury of experimenting with new ideas." They might not say these things in exactly these ways. Nonetheless, these feelings are present and they tell a story—it's a dreadful story. They have lost hope and they are growing more comfortable with "the known" each passing day. They keep saying "no" to their imagination and their desire to stay up to date. But these people don't have to be this way.

The possibilities for making ongoing change and improvement by tapping into our creative energies reside within each one of us. We are meant to be active, creative beings. One way to be your own worst enemy is to submit to the forces that tie you to dull, established, and out-of-date practices—routines and procedures that choke your creative abilities. Another way people become their own worst enemy is not to look for other avenues for creative expression outside of the workplace when none exist within it. Many people who are unable to exercise the full range of their imagination's powers in the workplace derive genuine and lasting satisfaction applying these capabilities elsewhere—outside of their work. The important thing is that they do not let their minds corrode.

Consider what you do day to day. Ask yourself what it is that holds you back from doing a better job. Notice what it is that limits you or makes you grumpy and bored. No doubt there are to be found in what you see patterns of mindless routine that don't make a hill of beans of difference to your effectiveness or provide you with any real satisfaction. And there is sure to be found, in what you discover by going through this simple exercise, a handful of problems that you've been meaning to get around to and fix. But, like that pile of junk you've been meaning to clear out of your garage for the past few years, there hasn't been time for you to do it. And if there were any time, something more important or inviting has likely taken precedence. We all have the proverbial "leaking faucets and squeaky doors" where we work. We put up with these nuisances for "just a little bit longer" because we feel too busy with other problems to do anything about them now. Unproductive routines or effectiveness-cheating nuisances, like house guests who have worn out their welcome, stay . . . and stay. To break the chains of these mindless routines we need to face not just the problems themselves but ourselves as well. Devoting time to them is only half the battle. The other half is to look for ways to be clever, imaginative, and creative persons ourselves.

An undeniable aspect of the world in which we live is that people are busy making changes. New ideas are continually being dreamed up and applied. Some of these ideas flop. Others produce marginal improvements. But some others yield astounding benefits. In hotly competitive economies, such as ours, the winners are usually those who are quickest to adopt the latest and most beneficial improvements. These improvements may involve getting better returns from marketing efforts, squeezing added fuel efficiencies from heating and air-conditioning systems, or driving down the numbers of defective parts produced. Whatever the new ideas or advancements might be, those individuals or organizations that adopt them to their benefit will usually beat out those who do not, those who remain chained to obsolete methods.

One effective way to break with entrenched methods and make improvements is to set specific improvement goals. If you think about it, you will quickly realize that a host of nagging problems seem to linger within organizations themselves—the approval processes for making changes are too cumbersome, the ways meetings are scheduled and conducted lead to wasted time, the procedures for getting information passed between production and accounting and the sales personnel lead to delays and inconsistencies of actions. These sorts of problems could be attacked and many of them solved reasonably effectively. What is true for organizations in terms of problems that need to be solved and opportunities for improvement, is also true for ourselves, as individuals. If we were totally honest, each one of us could identify problems in the ways we perform our work. Each of us could make improvements in ourselves. The idea suggested here is to set goals in the following four areas: (1) problems to be solved in your organizational unit; (2) improvements in the ways your organizational unit performs its functions; (3) problems to be solved in your performance; and (4) improvements you could make in yourself to be a better performer.

The Challenge to Be Creative

Although our next story occurred long ago, the lesson it teaches is every bit as relevant to us now as it was then. Many years ago there was a company that designed and manufactured diesel engines for industrial applications. This company had a problem: its sales were slipping. The firm was losing contracts to its rivals. Top management responded in the usual ways by pressuring marketing personnel to make more sales and production employees to cut costs. The management's response was to follow the same simple approach it had always used to boost the bottom line—sell more at a lower price and cut expenses to make up the difference. Sales personnel responded accordingly. They sharpened their order-writing pencils and cut very good deals for buyers, accepting orders at rock-bottom prices—mostly from customers who had special needs and who ordered only a few rather than hundreds of any particular engine model at a time. To make these special models would require custom designs. This requirement translated into increased work for the company's engineers, who were responsible for creating engine designs for the operating conditions specified by the buyers. It meant more design requests with less time to complete each one. Additionally, to cut costs and save money on expensive revisions, management pressured designers to come up with ideas that did not have to be modified or changed once prototype engines were made and tested.

More orders with varied requirements meant more design requests and added the pressures of having to be "right" the first time. What did all these pressures produce? Lackluster designs. Engineers stuck with the tried and true designs that were not as advanced as those rival firms were turning out. The reasons for unimaginative designs were clear: time pressures and the need for engines manufactured from these new designs to work right the first time they were built. What else could these engineers do under such pressures but turn to designs that had worked in the past? They used the same basic ideas that they were sure would work and that they knew they could complete within the short time frame given them. But that wasn't the end of the story. While this firm continued to lose out to its competitors, the engineers who worked there grew increasingly bored and frustrated with their jobs and with themselves. They knew that they had creative talents that were not being used. The engineers felt that their jobs were not challenging. Worse still, they realized that they were growing obsolete in their field. The best engineers left for other positions, and eventually the firm was bought out by a rival.

Many jobs are structured in ways that choke off the possibilities for creativity. Yielding to time pressures to get work out discourages original thinking. In many jobs the unspoken message is: "We don't want you to think," "We want you to do exactly as you are told. And we want you to do it quickly, and over and over again." Monotony, boredom, alienation—these are the results of mindless jobs. What can a person who is stuck in one of these jobs do about it? How does one rise above the mind-deadening routine? How can people exercise their God-given freedom to create?

Ignite Your Inborn Imagination

Consider civilization's achievements—its architecture, literature, atomic power, democracy, space travel, prescription drugs, refrigeration, canned soup. These did not come into being by acts of nature but by acts of human beings. Something independent of the world's natural forces is alive and active in our world. It is a possibility that is born in all of us. It is our capacity to imagine and to act on our own choosing. Human desire to understand the mysteries of our universe and the desire to harness their powers for our benefit is the driving force behind much of the change that goes on in our world. The human qualities that enable people to do this—to follow their curiosity, to use their imagination, to try to control their environment—are not things humans gave themselves. These gifts are ours to use if we are but curious, study hard, think imaginatively, and risk putting them into concrete forms. Without freedom and imagination, humans would be condemned to a state of monotonous repetition. We would not be the creatures we understand ourselves to be. Human nature is inseparable from creativity. We instinctively seek to impose our will on the natural order, altering it, adding to it. It calls us to expand ourselves, to use our originality to defeat unthinking habit. And, in responding to these calls, we enter higher levels of mental evolution.

If you look deeply enough into yourself, you will find two powerful urges: (1) your curiosity and (2) your desire for self-determination. Humans are free to choose between being active and being passive. We can choose whether we will use our powers of wonderment and curiosity to seek answers to questions or allow our minds to rest and not to put pressure on them to think. We can be active, thinking individuals or passive observers of our surroundings. Unlike members of the animal kingdom, we are not limited by the instincts implanted by nature. It is not the robin but the instinct that nature put in the robin that guides it to build its nest each spring in the shape it does. The robin does not create: it yields to nature's predetermined and unchanging call. In marked contrast to animals, we have the capacity to think, to understand, to control our actions, to imagine. We are free to move beyond our innate urges and instincts. We can be creative.

This is one of the most fundamental choices humans can make. How we choose will affect what we ultimately contribute to the world and what we experience in the way of personal satisfaction.

You don't need to be a nuclear physicist or a literary genius to exercise your creative powers. Just keep your mind active and seek to make improvements. The woman who develops a method for preparing low-cholesterol Alfredo sauce by substituting chicken broth, strained yogurt, corn starch, and other ingredients for butter and flour and cream, is being creative. It has been said, and for good reason, that a first-rate soup reflects more creativity than does a third-rate play. The world of work offers unlimited opportunities for thoughtful men and women to use their imaginations, to apply their problem-solving skills, to be clever, to create. The salesperson who thinks of a different way for attracting customers, the service mechanic who devises better methods for identifying the causes of malfunctioning equipment, the clerical person who comes up with new approaches for saving supplies can all be said to be creative—and so can you.

Free Yourself to Use Your Imagination

If you are serious about wanting to break the dams upstream that prevent useful ideas from flowing downstream, you need to eliminate the assumptions and habits that choke off creative ideas. The secret of the creative person is that he defeats the forces that bind him to monotony, repetition, and mindless conformity. To become more creative you will need to free your creative abilities and use them. A good place to start is with your curiosity. Learn to set it free. Welcome opportunities to be curious and let the urges within you to see more, to know more, and to understand more, grow freely.

An excellent illustration of a person who pursued his curiosity appeared recently in a *Fortune* magazine article about a man named Paul Ewald, a professor at the University of Louisville. He has been at the forefront of understanding how disease spreads and kills. Professor Ewald's research has led to a number of startling conclusions, many of which seem to conflict with conventional wisdom. For one thing, Dr. Ewald urges more thoughtful uses of antibiotics. Their overuse fosters the rise of antibiotic-resistant bacteria. The more virulent strains multiply with greater ease and more rapidly after medicines eliminate their competitors within the body.

Ewald's unorthodox approach to lessening the spread of resistant bacteria is to administer antibiotics to infected people only long enough to let their natural immune systems kick in and eliminate the culprits. The idea is to allow the superior powers of the human body's own defense mechanisms to work as they have evolved to work. Over millions of years, evolution has given human beings superior germ-fighting powers that resist infectious microorganisms. Should you take aspirin to lower a fever? Most people do; it makes them feel better. But Ewald's research suggests it might be better to allow the body to "do its own thing"—fight off the invading virus naturally. It has long been known that the elevated fever response to invading viruses has evolved over the millennia to fight off germs. Studies on reptiles and mammals suggest that rising body temperatures—a response mechanism that has evolved in humans—lower the risk of death from respiratory infections, because many germs cannot live in the heat. During the cough and cold season, Ewald conducted a study with his students. Those who went to bed and stayed there as soon as they felt a cold coming on, allowing their natural immune systems to give their fullest energies to fighting germs, recovered within twenty-four hours. Those who kept going, popping pills along the way, took an average of ten days to beat their colds.

These and other scientific breakthroughs had their beginning when, as a graduate student at the University of Washington in 1977, Paul Ewald came down with a bug. Up until that time he was interested in studying the social behavior of sparrows. When an intestinal virus entered his body and gave him a bad case of diarrhea, an interesting set of questions entered his mind. Lying in his sickbed Ewald wondered, *What is diarrhea good for?* "I started thinking maybe it's a defense mechanism by the body to get rid of an infectious agent. But in an argument with myself, I realized that it might be due to a microbe manipulating my body in order to spread itself." Diarrhea—is this condition the strategy tiny microbes use to survive? Do these tiny microbes create diarrhea as a way to find fresh victims to live on through the contamination of hands, objects, and water supplies? That thought led Ewald to forget about sparrows and pioneer a branch of medicine that analyzes disease from the perspective of evolutionary biology. Invigorated by having his own set of questions to sort through, Ewald began trying to understand infections. Library research led him to uncover countless studies on infectious microbes, studies that reached many conflicting conclusions. By arguing with himself as to the meaning and significance of these many studies, Ewald arrived at his own set of conclusions. These appeared in a landmark paper he published in *The Journal of Theoretical Biology* in 1980. In it he identified a list of tricks that microbes have evolved to exploit their hosts, as well as countermeasures hosts have developed to fight back.

Let's summarize the ways in which Professor Ewald reached his scientific breakthroughs. This overview will give us useful guidelines for how we might tap our powers of originality.

- He followed his curiosity where it led him. His mind was hospitable to questions to which he did not yet have answers. In a sense, he had a childlike open mind to things, shown by his capacity to wonder, his ability to raise questions about things he did not understand, his being comfortable with not knowing things, and his yearning to learn more about them—which he did.

- He was his own man, not a person driven to do what others expected of him. He explored what he saw as being interesting. Who else would spend time studying the social behavior of sparrows but someone comfortable with what interests him? He was unconcerned with what others might think or say.

- He went to work on a real problem. It was a question that arose from a real situation. He did not wall himself off from reality and say to himself, "I'm going to make myself a creative person who comes up with new ideas." In fact he was not concerned about making himself more creative in the abstract sense. Instead, he went to work on a real problem to solve. He asked difficult questions and then set about finding answers to them.

- He prepared his mind, filling it with information found in every study and experiment he could read. To him creative effort involved many years of learning. He believed that he could, through careful thought and hard work, arrive at a better understanding of something that he wanted to know more about. He believed in his abilities.

- He did not judge possible explanations too hastily, grabbing hold of some immediately and rejecting others altogether. Rather, he kept his mind open to explanations as to how things work, how nature functions. His inquiring urge overcame his judging urge. He thought long and hard about how to make ideas into provable conclusions. He was not prone to give up on possible explanations because they appeared far-fetched at first glance.

- He was receptive to insights when they entered his mind, but didn't stop there. He pushed forward to verify them. He argued with himself as to whether his speculations were or were not valid. He tested his hypotheses. He turned crude ideas and incomplete explanations into provable ideas and complete explanations through rethinking every part and detail.

Be Hospitable to Your Curiosity

The other day we noticed a class of second-graders on a field trip. Their teacher and two parents had their hands full trying to keep track of these energy-filled, busy, curious seven-year-olds. Nothing, as far as we could tell, escaped their attention. One was examining blades of grass; another was down on her knees watching an insect move about in the dirt; two other boys were examining cloud formations and telling each other what the shapes of these clouds reminded them of—and they began making up stories. The entire world lay before these youngsters and they were taking it all in and enjoying all the varied delights before them.

We wondered why the adults passing by the class appeared so bored. No doubt the older people who were outdoors that day were consumed with worries and plans and things like housecleaning, bill paying, undone errands on their "to do" list, and work matters. The contrast between the enthusiasm level of the children and the adults nearby made us realize something simple, yet terribly important. The children were perfectly comfortable being who they were, children. Unlike the adults, who tried to appear knowledgeable and in control, the children accepted their ignorance but did not rest with it. They were eager to learn more about their world. They were open to the many mysteries that lay before them. The lesson we arrived at from what we observed is that humility allows a person to step into the unknown and to learn. The creative person humbly admits his ignorance. It is the childlike quality of curiosity that leads a person to question. And in trying to find answers to these questions one is led to uncover new knowledge and find untried solutions and to test them.

In preparing this chapter we examined the biographies of many of the world's great creative geniuses. What we found in our research was actually rather simple. The common thread that runs through all their lives is the urge to find solutions to problems that challenged them.

Creators have an uncanny capacity to frame problems in clever ways and then find answers to them.

Another dimension of creative people is their desire to express themselves in ways that their sensitivities urge them to do. Ideas have a way of welling up in these people to the point that they have to be expressed. And so, as the songwriter walks down a street, tunes fill his thoughts inexplicably and another inner force urges him to write them down. A scientist sees phenomena everywhere he looks and his mind is flooded with questions that evoke more questions and finally more penetrating insights are born, which he is moved to express. We hear so often that creativity requires our inner child to escape. The advice that follows from this is that we ought to become more like the child we all once were. There is a child within each of us and that child can be curious and blurt out, as children often do, whatever it occurs to them to say. It is this very quality of unpretentiousness, of being naive, that enables a person to give free rein to her freedom to express her ideas freely and be creative because of it. But we also need to be more adult, more responsible in following through with all the hard work that's needed to take a rough, unpolished idea and develop it into a proven, well-thought-out and complete creation.

Be Your Own Person: Express Yourself

Our desire to fit in and receive approval from others frequently conflicts with our willingness to express our individuality and stand out from the crowd. From early on, most of us are rewarded more for conforming to the expectations of others—our parents, teachers, friends—than we are for our individuality. This is one reason why conformity takes root in people's lives early on, when they are in school. This has both positive and negative consequences. Think about it. For one thing, we are made to learn things we need to know. Education stresses intake, retention, and application. To achieve these aims quickly and uniformly teachers tell students what to think. Learners are rewarded for listening attentively and remembering. Tests measure how much the learners recall, how well they remember details and facts, and how closely they follow prescribed routines. Typically, this is what passes for education. But what is it that's been learned? It is sterile information, data, theories, facts—not how to think, how to create.

The negative consequence of conformity-focused education, that stresses information retention, is that it fails to teach lessons that are most needed if one is to thrive in a rapidly changing world. This method of education fails to develop the ability and inclination to think independently, to be curious, to be creative. Give those youngsters a problem to solve who have been long exposed to classroom instruction where teachers tell, and they are lost. They will wait passively with polite but blank expressions on their faces, expecting their teacher to tell them what to do and how to do it, step by step. Look into their hearts and you will find that the deepest fear these youngsters have is being unable to give the "right" answer and thus looking bad in the eyes of others.

Instead of ridding students of the forces and habits that choke off creativity, we find just the opposite taking place in schools today. If you wonder why creativity is so rare in many lives, talk to students—particularly older students in colleges and universities. Ask them what they find most threatening and difficult. They will likely tell you, "courses in which the professor does not tell us the answers, courses in which assignments are vague and where we have to dig the answers out for ourselves." Ask them how they think teachers should teach and they will say, "They should just tell us the answers." In effect, these students are saying that they want to be told what to think and how to think. In their hearts you will find them asking their teachers, "Don't make me think." "Tell me the steps to follow for getting to the right solution." They have these wants because these students are more driven to feel good about themselves by doing well in a safe and predictable environment than they are by their own natural curiosity, which is being extinguished by the system that is supposedly educating them. How different these attitudes are from the person with confidence in his imagination who says, "I can do this on my own."

A man named E. Paul Torrance, who was director of the Bureau of Educational Research at the University of Minnesota, once observed that society in general is downright savage toward creative thinkers, especially when they are young. Part of the reason, he said, is that educational systems must be coercive and emphasize the establishment of behavior norms. But must they also, in performing this useful function, squelch creativity? In his book, *Guiding Creative Talent*, Torrance tells of a fourth grade boy named Tom, who displayed exceptional creative talent. During an arithmetic lesson one day Tom questioned one of the rules in the textbook. This irritated the teacher. "So!" She said, "You think you know more than this book?"

Meekly, Tom replied that he didn't know more than the book, but he wasn't convinced that the rule made sense either. The teacher then asked the children to solve problems in their workbooks. Tom solved the problems easily and about as rapidly as he read them. The other children struggled. This upset the teacher all the more. Surely she wondered, *How did Tom get the correct answers doing the work in his own way?* The teacher could not handle Tom's independence any further. She demanded that he write down all of the steps that he went through to solve each problem.

Don't Wait Passively for Creative Ideas to Come to You

Wherever we find creativity, we almost always find it was the result of a person who willingly went to work on a real problem. Thomas Edison once remarked that "Everything comes to him who hustles." Work. Don't worry. That was Edison's advice. And he proved its usefulness by his own example. But despite Edison's experience and that of countless others who continue to make breakthroughs, there remains considerable mystery about how creative ideas actually come to people. When we read the words of people like Giacomo Puccini, that great operatic composer, who once remarked, "The music of this opera [Madame Butterfly] was dictated to me by God; I was merely instrumental in putting it on paper and communicating it to the public," what are we to think? Obviously, he and others feel as though they are merely the instrument through which creative energies are flowing. While it might have felt this way to Puccini, it is also evident that Puccini underestimated his own abilities.

One view of creativity is that it is something that comes to us like snowflakes falling from the sky. From this outlook arises a tendency to continue on in one's normal activities with little expectation for creative insights and the comforting belief that if a creative idea is going to come along, so be it, and if a creative idea is not going to come along, then so be that. You can be sure of one thing: those who wait for the perfect idea to pop into their thoughts complete and fully refined will invariably be disappointed. Creativity does not happen this way. Those who are creative find that the imaginative breakthroughs are the product of enormous effort. The smartest thing anyone can do to be more creative is to "get busy," and make extraordinary efforts to find answers to difficult problems.

It is far from true to say igniting creativity is like turning on a light bulb. Creative insights do not generally come whenever a person sits down and says to herself, "Now I am going to create something." Practically all creative ideas come when someone has a nagging problem—how can we get paint to adhere better to metal? How can we eliminate breakage in our shipments?—and then, usually unexpectedly, comes across a possible solution—a new technology, a different way of framing the problem, a long-neglected or hidden reality. It is when a person is alert to seeing the possibility that something just might provide a solution to the nagging problem that creativity is most likely to occur.

Our understanding of the creative process is deepened when we recognize that creativity is rarely a single event, although that's what people remember most about it. Many, perhaps most creations arise when a person puts pressure on his brain to solve a specific problem or find a way to fulfill a specific need. While it is true that creative ideas come to people unexpectedly, it is also true that these ideas rarely come to people who have not put pressure on their minds to work and think.

Many thoughtful people who have studied the creative act are in general agreement that it involves several aspects. First comes putting the conscious mind to work. We can think of this as "preparation," and it involves reading, studying, experiencing, facing problems, remembering information that might be useful whenever it is needed. The second aspect of creativity involves liberating the unconscious mind. This means making ourselves "receptive to solutions." Next comes trial and error experimentation phase, where ideas are generated, relationships examined, and possible answers or solutions to problems are examined. Lastly, the possible solutions presented are tested and verified, crude ideas refined, incremental improvements made; and they may be made again and again.

We put our conscious minds to work when we concentrate on a specific problem, when we define a problem that needs solving. The creative process also involves acting on the problem or question by first studying the situation. An excellent first step is to prepare yourself. This involves gathering all the knowledge about whatever it is that you are dealing with. It means mastering your subject.

How does one make himself receptive to creative ideas, seeing them for what they are, and recognize creative solutions to problems when they appear? This involves liberating the unconscious, which is far more complex and less straightforward than is putting the conscious mind to work. It involves being optimistic, ever hopeful of an answer, open to one's experiences, having tolerance for ambiguity, using one's capacity to shrug off mistakes and not worry excessively about the opinions of others, exercising the ability to toy with concepts, being "playful" with ideas, allowing one's inner-child side to explore and see new possibilities and to voice them freely. Liberation of the unconscious mind requires a willingness to allow the full powers of the mind to work in the ways they work best. This process may involve doing simple things such as giving oneself time so that creative ideas can be incubated and allowed to grow slowly, as they tend to do. Most important of all, it involves being able to recognize and welcome the solutions that flash into our conscious minds.

The incubation part of the creative process is where full powers of the unconscious work while the conscious mind rests, or goes elsewhere as we engage in different pursuits. One study showed that sleep, a good night of restful sleep, is one of the best ways for getting the unconscious to do its work. Other avenues of activity can also help the unconscious to work its magic. These include reading, travel, going for a walk, doing things out of the normal routine. Taking a long walk by oneself is usually very helpful, especially when one is in places that are quiet and free of distractions.

Illumination, the "Eureka!" moment, is when the conscious mind is signaled that a solution has arrived. This is the "ah ha!" feeling that occurs when an answer comes into one's consciousness. Frequently this occurs unexpectedly—while one is walking, reading, thinking about something else, seated in the theater or at church, looking at a waterfall or sunset. In a famous letter to a friend, Wolfgang Amadeus Mozart explained the excitement and delight he experienced when creative impulses swept through his mind. "All this inventing," he wrote, "this producing, takes place in a pleasing lively dream.... What has been produced I do not easily forget, and this is perhaps the best gift I have my divine Maker to thank for." From great scientists, artists, inventors, writers, we hear these same feelings expressed about the creative experience. They report a feeling of something from beyond themselves entering through them and taking form. Perhaps it is because this intensely uplifting and exhilarating feeling so dominates our beings that we are left with the false conclusion that some power beyond ourselves gave us the creative gift. It would be more accurate to think, however, that the gift of creativity is not any creative idea as such but is ourselves as beings with the capacity to be creative. It is up to us to choose to do so and that involves hard work.

Prepare Your Mind

The more varied your experiences are, the greater the likelihood becomes for creative sparks to ignite in your mind. Knowledge is the raw material of creativity. It has to be gathered, refined, digested, and organized. The more one knows and understands, the better become his chances to create, provided he willingly accepts challenges, goes to work on problems to solve, and keeps his mind free to think. The person who browses, reads, and engages in discussions that extend his understanding, particularly in ever-widening spheres, is more likely to create than the person who does not. Systematic study of the specific subject area in which a problem lies is a good first step to finding a creative solution to it. The more one masters her craft, the more she learns, understands and widens her horizons, the greater become her chances for arriving at a creative idea.

As a person goes through life reading, observing, learning through experiences, lessons and ideas begin to accumulate. Like a body of water dammed up, these ideas, lessons, and insights are stored in the memory. There they move about, each having the potential to encounter another and spawn further lessons, insights, ideas. Then one day, as this person wrestles with a problem or tries to compose a work of art, the flow of creative thoughts begins. Out they flow, as if the dam that had held them in place had been breached. They rush into this person's conscious mind and seem to be coming from powers far beyond and greater than this person believes her capabilities to be. Yet these ideas were there all along, stored away until a problem or creative challenge presented itself and needed expression.

Accept the Risks of Making Mistakes

Our safety-mindedness can be a good or a bad thing, depending on how we evaluate the situation. All too frequently our safety-mindedness cautions us against entertaining strange possibilities where it's not our life and health that could be in danger but our ego and self-esteem.

Fear of criticism causes ordinary people to do whatever it takes to spare themselves from looking foolish. Their worries go something like this: "Ought I to risk trying some new idea that might not work?" "Do I dare suggest an off-the-cuff idea in front of others, who might laugh at me?" "Do I dare make a mistake in front of others?" You have probably noticed how risk-avoiders operate: they skirt around anything that has a possibility of failure associated with it. They settle into routines devoid of novelty and challenge, they gravitate to the safe and easy. They engage in mind-numbing routines. They try to act smart and all-knowing. But, when they do speak, we find that their minds are capable of hatching little more than boring commentary.

If you want to be more creative here is a challenge you'll need to meet: swallow your fears, rise above your hesitations, and bravely go into battle with the unknown. The only result you can count on is that you will make mistakes. You'll have to make one mistake after another until a breakthrough comes and your raw idea is perfected into something useful and proves successful. Bob Halgrim, who began assisting Thomas A. Edison as a high school student in 1925, told the *Smithsonian Magazine* that working for Edison was a higher education in itself. Halgrin said that Edison was a common man with a lot of curiosity. Once the inventor told him, "I've made more mistakes than anyone who ever lived, but I wouldn't have done half as much if I hadn't made those mistakes."

Don't Be Made Uncreative by Your Judging Urge

No doubt at one time or another you have been in a meeting where someone suggested something and no sooner had the words left this person's lips than another person in the meeting voiced objections to it. The critic appears to know immediately why the idea is no good, why the suggestion cannot possibly work. Most of us have developed reflexes such as these that cripple creative ideas before they ever grow legs. Skepticism is sometimes useful; it can remove from further consideration wrongheaded suggestions. But more often than not, negative responses to ideas choke off possibilities that might grow into useful and productive breakthroughs. Creativity requires positive, open-minded attitudes, not negative, cynical ones. Whereas a negative person will examine an idea and think to herself, "How can I poke holes in this?" a positive person will greet that same idea as a source of possibilities and then go to work on adding to it, modifying it, imagining other variations it might take. If we ever want to be creative we need to develop our "possibilities urges" and discourage our "judgmental urges."

If you intend to make positive contributions to your organization, be positive yourself. It's always a good rule in life to remember that negative reactions often have a devastating effect, particularly on those who have not developed their creative abilities. Also, keep in mind that whatever the proposed idea is someone can always show it to be wrong, unworkable, illogical. Clearly it is easier for people to find fault with something than it is for them to find the seeds of useful possibilities within it. A sad reality is that most of us have become highly sophisticated at being judgmental, while we are woefully lacking in taking raw ideas and distilling out of them valuable benefits. What lies behind our tendency to be more judgmental than the possibility developers? One reason we develop in this way is that we feel that we move up or down the scale of other people's opinions of us by what we appear to know. But the only way we know how to do this is to find fault with things and cynically proclaim the defects we see in others and their ideas. Of course there are weaknesses and faults to be found—they exist in everything and everyone. Another reason for our judgmental tendencies is that we are more politically oriented than we are results-oriented. By this we mean that we seem to be more concerned with advancing ourselves and our own points of view than we are with achieving beneficial results. We tend to be more concerned with who wins and who receives credit than we are with contributing to progress. Because we act in these ways, we severely limit our creative possibilities. The simple truth is that those who have excessive faith in their own ideas and who rigidly guard them are unfitted to make discoveries.

All Good Ideas Need Polishing

Most creative ideas come into our mind much like a newborn moose enters the world, ugly, gangling, scarcely able to stand up on its own legs. We can barely see them even when we know what to look for and try hard to find them. They are just too ugly and unrefined to be noticed for what they are. Like seeds tossed upon bare ground, most creative ideas never get the benefit of fertile conditions where they can sprout and grow. Instead, they are blown away and left to dry and wither. It is vitally important that new ideas receive attention just after they appear if ever they are to develop a life of their own. It is after the birth moment that the work of creativity needs the most careful work—reshaping and polishing the untested rough thoughts and reorganizing them, making them into something that can stand up on its own.

Hearing creative geniuses like Sir Isaac Newton, who suddenly glimpsed a theory of gravity from observing an apple drop from a tree, we blithely conclude that their creative ideas simply came to them from above, like a falling apple. But Newton was accustomed to thinking about what he observed. He was gifted at asking himself relevant questions that led him to penetrate some of nature's deepest mysteries: Was the apple being attracted to earth? Or could the earth have been attracted to the apple? Or, maybe, each object was attracting the other. Newton's real contribution to civilization, his mathematical explanation of the gravity phenomenon, was developed by him later after many hours of mental work.

Behind every creative breakthrough there always stands a person or persons who willingly experimented. This is why it's smart to make yourself into a person who gladly and optimistically tries out one possibility after another, sorting out the workable from the unworkable, the useful from the vast sea of the useless. Your creative possibilities will be enriched whenever you work diligently and continue to say to yourself, "This isn't good enough. I can make it better." When you do this, you'll become someone who will face failed attempts but who also learns from them and slowly refines raw ideas into useable solutions. You'll grow and develop more confidence because of your increasing competence. Optimism and improvement-mindedness are important aspects of creativity because many creative ideas are hatched while someone is experimenting and exploring for new possibilities. Many creative breakthroughs have arisen because someone was authentically interested in finding out more about something or was trying to make improvements to something that already worked. It wasn't the rewards that drove these people so much as it was their genuine interest in something they were trying to understand or perfect.

Creativity is not alone a process of accepting great ideas but more a process of developing ordinary ideas into great ideas. Scientific breakthroughs and advancements are not solely the product of keen insight—that is merely a beginning point—but the result of painstaking and backbreaking toil. Insight and imagination are gifts we receive from our subconscious minds. It's up to us then to turn these flashes of insight into concrete advancements through steady effort. But there will always be setbacks and failures along the way. Those who are highly creative see these setbacks and disappointments as valuable lessons to build upon. As Edison was once reported to have remarked, "I have discovered a thousand ways not to make a light bulb."

Consider also what else occurs through this repeated process of perfecting. An artist tries to create a certain mood in a painting and the first several tries fail to capture the intended emotions. But each time the artist comes up short of his aim, another spark of creativity ignites, new ideas enter his mind, different ways of accomplishing his purpose present themselves. As if by magical forces, different approaches mysteriously appear. Think of trick birthday cake candles that reignite after the celebrant blows them out. This is much like what happens in the mind of the artist whose spark of imagination turns to a flame again after each failure leading him to try another approach. The artist is challenged but does not retreat in defeat. The failures lead the artist to create many possible solutions that would otherwise have been unimaginable. The artist meets failure, but the result is not discouragement and hostility but a renewed sense of creative adventure. By the flow of creative solutions that keep coming into her mind, the artist knows her inner voice is saying to her, "Keep trying. Keep learning from your failures. Don't give up. Risk making mistakes and accept the consequences of trying. And, above all, press on."

BECOME AN EFFECTIVE LEARNER AND CONTINUE LEARNING

Be Curious, Reflect on Your Observations, Expose Your Mind to New Ideas

"Being ignorant is not so much a shame as being unwilling to learn."

Benjamin Franklin

One of our students, a man named Bill who was taking the last course for his MBA degree when we knew him, demonstrated a valuable inner strength, the ability to learn from on-the-job experiences. Bill worked for the Richardson Baking Company of Indiana. After eight years' experience, he had worked his way up to the position of director of operations. Company sales came from products that relied on two different types of production. The first was fairly simple and had been performed many times in the same ways over many decades. The second type was highly automated, high volume, and precise in nature. Outside consultants engineered the second type of production process. They prepared specific procedures that were to be followed exactly as specified. These procedures were spelled out in a manual and followed closely by members of Bill's department. Bill's success with running established production lines for eight years problem-free gave him the false impression that his firm could produce anything it wanted to with relative ease. He felt that all that his firm needed to do to earn more would be to get more business and bake more products. As long as they kept following the specified procedures, Bill thought they'd be successful.

An opportunity to expand operations arose one day, and Bill's company jumped at it. But the change proved Bill wrong about what he had come to believe. When Richardson Baking contracted to produce a newly developed cracker for the retail market, Bill thought that all he and his employees would need to do would be to "follow the specified procedures." The first batches of crackers were a colossal failure. Part of the difficulty stemmed from the fact that the cracker was very thin, which made it difficult to handle without breaking. This problem made it impossible for line employees to package the cracker in the customary way. Another source of the problem was the specifications themselves. Following them precisely proved more difficult than anticipated. This meant that Bill and those in his department had a constant struggle to follow complex procedures. For months low production levels, low yields, mediocre quality, and frequent equipment breakdowns plagued Bill's department. If they wanted to achieve profitability with the cracker-baking contract, Bill and his employees would have to learn new ways of baking, handling, and packaging the product.

To his credit, Bill is no quitter. He is not one to be easily discouraged. With failure staring him in the face, he turned to his best and most experienced people for help. Together, they committed themselves to making the new product successful. They tackled the production difficulties one at a time, learning from their mistakes and intermittent successes. Gradually, as they went along, they learned. Working round the clock, Bill's people noticed every good thing and every bad thing that happened as they tried different ways of making the crackers. As they worked, they asked themselves questions as to what was behind things going right and things going wrong. They tried some things that worked, which was good. But it wasn't always good enough to suit them, so they then asked themselves, "How can we make it work even better?" In time they got the cracker-baking line up and running. Everyone contributed something to the effort—if not a winning suggestion, at least support, enthusiasm, and good questions. Their minds challenged by real problems, the baking unit responded with real solutions which they tried out and revised as needed. Trial and error was the order of the day; no one got scolded for making mistakes—these would be turned into valuable lessons to be catalogued and used to guide future actions. The team worked diligently and intelligently. Because they worked so hard, they learned. And what they learned, they implemented. Eventually they mastered how to bake these delicate crackers. Through their learning they turned a losing proposition into a profitable one.

Learning: A Natural Activity of Humans, an Essential Element in Our Work

If you would like to know what enables certain people to move ahead and do well with new challenges, take a look at their superior ability to learn. Whether we are concerned with earning a living or just with living our lives, learning is one of the main keys to our success and satisfaction. We learn throughout our lives. Some of us learn more than others and some of us are better learners than others. But we all learn. Just as there are all kinds of things one can learn, there are also all kinds of ways in which humans learn. Perhaps many of the ways in which we are different can be explained in part by what we have learned and by the ways in which we have learned what we know how to do.

Think of all the things one needs to know in order to perform work effectively: how to carry out each activity, how to get the information needed to perform tasks well, how to get along with others—there are so many things one needs to know how to do. But other things we need to learn are not easily apparent. New processes require new procedures. These in turn require new learning. New products are constantly coming out, not to mention the servicing procedures for them—all of which require learning. Technology changes and we need to keep up to date. There are always new people to work with, changes in our organization's structure, different competitors invading our firm's territories—all these demand that we keep learning. If you expect to move ahead, into better paying, more demanding positions, you'll need to learn.

Clearly, learning involves more than just memorizing of facts and information. It involves developing the imagination and strengthening the will as well. Humans are capable of taking in abstract concepts, ideas, and applying them to particular circumstances that might never have been imagined before. We want to melt the right amount of paraffin to seal the glass containers in which we plan to store our homemade jam. How much paraffin do we need? It's simple. We measure the diameter of the jars and use formulas from geometry to compute the exact volume. Learning how to solve novel problems using abstract concepts is a far more complex phenomenon than mere conditioning.

It involves the use of one's imagination to see possibilities for the use of ideas and the application of one's will to choose to apply them. What's more astounding about the ability humans have to learn is their capacity to learn from their own experiences and to create ideas that explain events. In other words, this is the ability each person possesses to create theories about how the world operates and to form explanations of cause and effect relationships.

Ideas, information, and experiences—these are taken in by humans in varying degrees, depending on the nature of their perceptivity. What one perceives has the potential to affect that person. The extent of that affect will be determined by several things: (1) what other ideas or information the person can recall; (2) the nature of the person's imagination; and (3) the person's will to think and apply effort in creative and useful ways. Unfortunately and all too often, humans have developed self-limiting beliefs, attitudes, and habit patterns that choke off further learning and lead their minds and hearts down paths of rigidity and stagnation. They are mired in ruts of sameness. One of the main purposes of this chapter is to identify those self-limiting attitudes, beliefs, and habits that curtail our thirst for learning and prevent us from developing our minds and skills to their fullest.

What to Do When Learning a New Skill

Imagine yourself as a beginner. It might be that you are new to a job and need to learn how to operate a piece of machinery or make sales calls. It might be that you are starting out in an entry-level position that involves multiple tasks, not repetitive ones such as those performed by people working on an assembly line. Or it might be that what you are is a beginner at something outside of work, like golf. It really doesn't matter what it is that you are learning to do for the first time. The essential steps and conditions for effective learning are much the same. And the steps for teaching beginners tend to follow the same general principles. Let's consider what these steps are and what learners can do for themselves to speed up their learning.

Acknowledge What You Know and What You Don't Know. Any novice is wise to acknowledge at the outset what she knows and does not know, what she is able to do well and what she is not able to do as well. An effective trainer will want to build on what the learner already knows and not waste time or destroy enthusiasm by going over what is already mastered. Even if you do know the basics, it is generally helpful to review them. It is always possible that you may have forgotten an important element or that what you think you know is actually dead wrong.

In this stage of the learning process an astute instructor will ask questions that require more than simple "yes" or "no" responses. Questions like, "Do you know how to operate this kind of machine?" or "Can you cause a golf ball to go in the direction you want it to go?" may yield misleading information to instructors. Wanting to appear smart and unwilling to admit to deficiencies, many people will answer these sorts of questions in the affirmative. To get around these difficulties an astute instructor will find out what you know by asking open-ended questions such as, "Tell me how this machine works; explain what the controls on it do and how one should use them." Better still, the instructor can get an even more accurate understanding of where the learner is by asking that learner to demonstrate how to hit a golf ball or operate a machine, or perform whatever it is that the person is supposed to learn. It is useful for the instructor to understand what a learner's knowledge and ability levels are right away. Learners will help themselves greatly if they are totally honest with their instructor as to what they know and understand. As humans, we all want to feel good about ourselves but this causes many of us to tend to have an inflated estimation of our level of understanding and abilities. We make ourselves our own worst enemy whenever we do this.

Overcome Fears. Every good teacher knows that learning moves ahead faster and on a surer footing when the right kind of encouragement is provided to nervous learners. Fear of failure and self-doubts are ever-present obstacles and the more directly they are faced for what they are, the better the chances are that they will be dealt with effectively. Anyone who has begun a new job, just like every small child going off to school for the first time, knows the tensions that are felt when facing the unknown. The unknown can be daunting: "Will I do okay?" "Will I fit in?" "Will others, especially the higher-ups in positions of power and authority, like me?" "Will I succeed?" These are normal concerns and it is always best to admit their existence. No matter whether one is beginning at the bottom of an organization or starting out day one as the president of the United Sates, these same kinds of questions and worries are present. We are but human and we all wonder quietly, sometimes secretly, *Will I do okay?*

It is extremely important for both instructors and learners to face up to the fear that accompanies entry into the unknown. Left unchecked, fears can quickly turn into anxieties. Fear is something you know about: you can identify its source. You generally have a fair idea as to how to deal with a specific fear. Anxiety is "fear" plus "confusion." Now you haven't a clue as to what to do in the face of your fear, making you like the proverbial deer caught in the headlights of a fast-moving automobile. It freezes in place, unable to run. How can one escape the paralyzing grip of anxiety? That was the question a group of researchers asked themselves many years ago as they studied how best to handle new hires at Texas Instruments. What they found and later reported in an article appearing in the *Harvard Business Review* was that immediate supervisors could help new employees learn faster and make fewer mistakes by reducing their level of anxiety.

The experimenters did four things to reduce anxiety. (1) They told trainees that their opportunity to succeed was very good, that they all had what it took to learn how to perform the tasks satisfactorily; (2) they told trainees to disregard hall talk, the hazing rumors spread about by veteran employees. One rumor the veterans used on newcomers was that over half of all new employees are fired for poor performance, something that led directly to high levels of anxiety; (3) they urged trainees to talk to their supervisor, to ask questions. Supervisors realize that new employees need constant instruction and learning technical terminology takes time; and (4) they told trainees, "Get to know your supervisor." This step made supervisors seem less threatening, more "helpers" than "judgers of performance."

These four measures produced astounding results. As anxiety levels went down, learning went up. Here are the specific outcomes: (1) Training time was shortened by one half; (2) training costs were lowered to one third their previous levels; (3) absenteeism and tardiness dropped to one half of the previous normal; (4) waste and rejects were reduced to one fifth their previous levels; and (5) training costs overall were cut by as much as 15–30 percent.

Individuals themselves can place several useful thoughts into their minds to overcome their fears of failure and reduce anxiety. Practically every automobile driver can remember the fear associated with the driving test they had to take to get their first driver's license. The list of worries was long: "Will I pass the test?" "Am I going to make too many mistakes?" "Will they flunk me for being unable to parallel park?" "Will I forget some obscure traffic law and fail because I broke a law?" "Will the test-giver be too tough on me and make me nervous?"

It is always good advice to face fears of failing and similar worries head-on. Go ahead, admit your fears when you experience them. Once they have had their say, you can get on with what's important, the learning. Let's say that you are worried about whether you can pass a driver's test. You might fear that you will fail. To deal with fears like this one say to yourself, "If all the people I see driving cars today were able to pass this test, why shouldn't I be able to pass it too?" Realizing that others who have succeeded are not any smarter or better than you are will frequently give you the reassurance needed that you too can succeed. Another useful way to reduce fear and anxiety is to review your previous accomplishments and recognize that you have done reasonably well with other challenges. You might try saying to yourself, "This challenge is not all that different from other things that I have already succeeded at." It is easy to make yourself your own worst enemy by dwelling on fears and letting them overwhelm you. Many a fine performer has suffered the embarrassment of giving a terrible performance because they gave in to their worries, allowing them to grow uncontrollably large.

Follow the Prescribed Steps Carefully. Now let's consider the things that spell the difference between performing a new skill reasonably well early on and failing repeatedly at performing it effectively. In the next stage of the learning process, instructors will show and explain the steps to be followed. What should you do during this phase? We have four suggestions: (1) Pay close attention to what the instructor shows you and tells you. This is no time to let your mind wander or drift off. Notice the details and catalog all the steps and suggestions in your memory. It may sound trivial and oversimplified to say this, but the main factor in learning is, simply, paying attention. So, focus on what is being taught. (2) Ask questions. Too many people are afraid to ask questions because they want to avoid being seen as ignorant or dumb. This is always a huge mistake. Of course learners don't know what's being taught. That's precisely why they are receiving instruction. Good instructors are never bothered by good, sincere questions. What bothers them are learners who don't care. Actually instructors find questions helpful, because they provide strong indicators that you want to learn. Moreover, your questions are also helpful reminders to your instructor of things that need emphasis. Your questions also provide check points as to where you are in your understanding. Be assured that if you have a question, chances are excellent that others around you have the same question in their minds too. (3) Try to understand the thinking behind what you are doing. Sure, there are steps but what is the larger pattern behind them? Knowing why you are supposed to do certain things in prescribed ways is generally more important than knowing how to do these things. (4) Do what the instructor advises. This is not the time to think you are the expert—just "get with the program."

Application, Putting Ideas into Action. The next step in the learning process involves doing. The sooner this step begins, the more exciting and motivating it will be for the learner. We once heard about a basketball coach who lectured a group of nine-year-old boys on the rules of the game for nearly an hour before getting down to playing on the first day of a basketball camp. We can easily imagine the frustration felt by those youngsters and how little of the instructor's lecture ever stuck in their minds. In the doing phase of the learning process the learner swings the golf club, takes hold of the boat's tiller and steers, grasps the wheel of the automobile and presses down on the accelerator pedal. If the instructor is nearby, this is a good time to demonstrate each step as you perform it. In doing anything—particularly for the first time—it is generally a good idea to be mindful of established rules. I (Charles) recall once when I was a freshman in high school. We were about to take our first algebra test and I was nervous. I wrote "Remember the Rules" atop my test paper. When the teacher returned my test the following week, I found that my teacher had circled this reminder to myself and had added a line: "Good advice!" Be guided by the rules. That's why they're called rules—because they work.

Naturally, everyone hopes to do well the first time out. This is understandable and healthy. But we've noticed an emotional difficulty that people have in the doing phase of learning, and it always causes them trouble. This difficulty begins with impatience. Impatience with one's self can be a good thing but only up to a point. This is because impatience with one's self in the face of a less than satisfactory performance frequently leads to anger. And when anger takes over, learning gets stuck in its tracks. Anger clouds one's judgment and concentration. It causes people to focus on the wrong things. Many things that people try to learn are hard to learn. We suggest you face this fact for what it is, a cold reality of life. Al Unser, Jr., two-time winner of the Indianapolis 500 race, put the matter this way. When an interviewer asked him about the difficulty of driving a race car, Unser said, "Of course, it is hard to drive a race car. If it were easy, everybody would be doing it."

Learn from Your Failures. We once observed young men in a college physical education class learning how to hit golf balls cleanly and straight. They were not having the success that they wanted. As they swung at their targets, some of their golf balls toppled off the tees and rolled a few short feet; other balls they struck veered off in directions these boys didn't intend for them to go. This made them mad. They swore at their clubs, their golf balls, themselves. And the more they swung and the more they missed their targets, the more they swore. Frustration and anger can hold anyone back from learning. Too many people have been ruined by well-meaning parents and teachers too eager to make them feel good about themselves. In trying to boost the self-esteem of youngsters, these adults have created the false impression that learning comes quickly and easily and that there is no such thing as failure, especially for them. But there *is* something called failure and it is very real. We are always better off when we don't view it as our enemy. The smart thing to do when it comes is to see it as a special kind of teacher. Your failures might be the most effective helper you can have. Indeed, if you ever find that even a hint of failure is completely absent when you are learning, be suspicious. Chances are good that you are either being deceived or are oblivious to shortcomings that are surely present. The person who admits to ignorance or to a lack of a skill takes the first step in learning.

One effective way for a person to meet failure head-on and make the most of it is to recognize a phenomenon called the learning curve. The idea behind the learning curve is easily illustrated by considering the relationship between the performance of a task and the accumulated experience of the person performing that task. Imagine the task of ironing a shirt. The first time a person irons a shirt it will take maybe fifteen to twenty minutes to get the job done well. Now fast forward several weeks and suppose this person has ironed a hundred shirts. Something happens to this person by way of the accumulated experiences of ironing. Speed increases because the person knows better how to handle the iron and learns better ways of performing the task. With this accumulated experience, it now takes the person maybe twelve minutes to iron a shirt. Move ahead in time and, with the added experience of a hundred more shirt ironings, the person performing the tasks has really "got it down." The time is reduced now to maybe eight minutes. Also, the person does a better quality job because of the accumulated experience. Understand the relationship between experience and performance. Practice, as the saying goes, makes perfect. People who understand these realities are better able to bear the disappointment of early failures than those who do not. Take heart in the knowledge that improvement comes with more practice and experience.

Another self-limiting tendency is defensiveness. A person's ego is always subject to threat in the face of failure, when he or she is not succeeding in learning a skill. It is at this point that knowledgeable instructors will show learners what the learner is doing wrong. Here again, pride and defensiveness can get in the way of good learning. One of our friends, named Phil, is a dog lover. He has had dogs all his adult life and likes to take them to obedience training classes where he learns from top-notch trainers how to train and discipline dogs. Phil told us about a time when the instructor corrected one of the other dog owners in the training class as to how to get his dog to do something that it wasn't doing. This owner had his own ideas about training his dog and wouldn't listen to the advice given by the expert. "My dog is different," the owner said. "Your suggestion won't work with him." The instructor shrugged her shoulders and tuned her attention to others in the class who were eager to learn what she had to teach them. When she corrected Phil on how to get his dog to do what he wanted, Phil listened and applied the instructor's advice. It worked. Phil was happy and his dog seemed happy too. The message here is clear: You cannot learn when you refuse to accept advice from someone who knows what she is talking about. So, don't let pride and defensiveness make you deaf to sound advice.

Learning New Job Duties

One of the most perplexing challenges that people confront in the workplace is change. Change is all around us, everywhere we look—and it is taking place all the time. As organizations change methods of operating to remain competitive, or move into new technologies, or begin making and marketing new products, change is the order of the day. New modes of operating, different forms of organization, new responsibilities, and varied working relationships—these are but some of the kinds of ways change can arrive. Change can also present itself whenever a person moves into a new position; adjusting to the demands and rigors of entirely different responsibilities is never easy. What many people fail to take into consideration is that change brings with it the need for learning. But frequently there is no one to teach the new ways of thinking, the new skills sets, the new priorities that the change demands. This is why each of us will do well to make learning— identifying what to learn and then learning it—a self-imposed responsibility. The person who makes herself an effective learner will do far better than the person who does not.

Consider the story of a man named Ronald, a diesel mechanic. Ronald's experience began over twenty years ago in Minnesota, where he learned his trade. Later, he and his wife moved west, where he took a position as a mechanic with a large construction company. He quickly became known as the expert to go to for help with difficult problems. Seeing his ability and the way younger mechanics looked up to him, management decided to promote Ronald to a supervisory position. In this capacity he was responsible for scheduling work, supervising mechanics, training them, and evaluating their performance. It was a job that required the skills of communication, human relations, organization, motivating—and there was paperwork too, which Ronald hated.

Ronald tried his best to comply with his boss's suggestions for how to organize and supervise those under him. He spent considerable time in an office. He didn't much care for the paperwork and planning. It was not long before Ronald could be found back on the shop floor, doing repair work himself. When his boss questioned Ronald about spending too much time doing the work instead of training and supervising others, his answer was always the same: "This is an especially difficult repair job and I'm the only one who knows how to handle it."

There are literally tens of thousands of people like Ronald to be found in workplaces. These are the people who have been promoted into positions of supervision but who cannot seem to make the adjustment from doing to supervising. They have derived security and satisfaction from being good at hands-on tasks for so many years that they have developed deeply ingrained self-images as being first-rate doers, which they are. Learning new responsibilities that demand different talents and skills for these people is difficult. This fact reveals a larger issue that needs to be understood for what it is, namely, that learning to perform complex functions also involves changing one's habits, perceptions, and attitudes. Humans are complicated creatures and not mechanical objects that can be adjusted or programmed to do different things merely by giving them information. They are social, emotional beings who have hearts and minds and imaginations. Learning therefore is best seen as an emotional experience and it is especially threatening and challenging to learners when their self-image, their pride, their habit patterns, their attitudes, and their beliefs and assumptions are challenged.

People will experience adjustment difficulties whenever they are promoted or transferred to different jobs, chiefly because different jobs require different skills, different habit patterns, and different priorities for using time. Understanding what one is supposed to do is one thing. Adjusting to different demands and performing different functions effectively is something else altogether. To make the needed adjustments and learn the new skills it is helpful to have the right sorts of inclinations and motivations. A person will not, for instance, suddenly become an effective communicator, or become a respectful and supportive team player, or become willing to put in long hours of painstaking attention to details, unless that person holds attitudes that are consistent with behaviors that are needed for effective performance in the different position. What's more, no matter how sound or useful these new behaviors and methods of performing work may seem, people simply will not be willing or able to follow new practices until they have learned about them, understood them, accepted them, and learned how to apply them.

Attitudes are not the cause of habits so much as they are the result of habits—that's what Harvard University philosopher William James concluded nearly a century ago. There is ample evidence to support his observation: the best way to alter one's attitudes is to first change one's habits, one's behaviors. We will take up the matter of self-discipline in a later chapter and revisit this idea in greater depth. But for now, let us simply recognize that attitudes matter and that when one learns about the different skills required for different assignments, it is essential to try to develop the right sorts of attitudes as one learns how to perform new skills.

Develop the Ability to Learn On Your Own

At the lowest levels of any organization, direction and guidance from one's immediate supervisor are the norm. But as a person settles into the day-to-day routine and shows the ability to carry out normally assigned tasks, the closeness of supervision lessens. At higher levels one is expected to act more independently. Bosses assign responsibilities and set goals and expect those responsible to figure out on their own how to accomplish the designated tasks. In today's fast-changing work environment, many assignments that individuals are asked to perform are unique. This makes it important for those who are assigned work to figure things out for themselves, to learn what needs to be done and find acceptable ways of doing it.

One of the most annoying and time-wasting things bosses encounter is the employee who constantly asks for precise directions as to how to carry out a piece of work. Young people sometimes make the mistake of demanding too much direction—they are really asking their boss to do their work for them. We once heard about a former student who created a very bad impression of herself in the mind of her boss by falling into this kind of behavior pattern.

Karla graduated with honors in accounting. We recall how pleased she was with herself when she accepted an offer from one of the top accounting firms. But unlike her professors, who were really more interested in getting Karla to like them than they were with teaching her to think for herself, her boss expected a far greater level of independence and maturity from Karla than she had developed. Her boss expected her to tackle difficult assignments on her own and, if she did not know something, to find out the answer for herself. When Karla didn't remember from her accounting classes exactly how to treat the odd circumstances she encountered, she went straightaway to her boss for answers—just as she had done the year before with her teachers in school. Her boss told her to go back and figure the problems out for herself. This offended Karla. In fact we learned that she complained to one of her friends that she thought her boss was tactless and rude. Part of the problem stemmed from the fact that Karla had never been expected to think for herself. She had never faced difficult problems where there was not "a correct, textbook" solution. In her attempts to feel good about herself by being the perfect student who always got the right answers, she missed the point of learning how to find reasonably good answers to real problems and get the job done.

It is a serious mistake, especially in today's changing world where new problems crop up because of rapidly altering conditions and circumstances, not to see the necessity for learning. Much of what you will need to learn in order to continue performing effectively you will have to learn for yourself, on your own. This is why the ideal is to make yourself strong and independent, able to size up situations and solve problems without irritating supervisors with childish demands for direction.

One of our MBA students, Mike Abrams of Cincinnati Financial, was a good bit more mature than Karla was and it worked to his benefit. Mike applied for a position in his company that he wanted and got it. His boss selected Mike from a pool of applicants precisely because he had developed a reputation for thinking and learning from his experiences. Now these qualities would be tested. Even though Mike had a degree in finance, he wasn't prepared for the job responsibilities he encountered. Indeed, what he ran into at work was considerably different from what he had learned in school. His boss heaped many responsibilities on Mike and expected him to get them done on his own.

At first Mike turned to his boss, the company's vice president, for guidance. But precise answers to how to do things—what Mike wanted and expected—didn't come. Mike's boss gave him only general guidance. After all, the boss was not about to take on a second job, Mike's. It wasn't until sometime later that Mike realized the motives behind his boss's methods: he wanted Mike to develop critical thinking and problem-solving skills on his own. It wasn't until several years had passed and Mike had developed into a successful professional that his boss told him why he had made Mike do things on his own. The boss wanted to find out where Mike's breaking point was. But Mike was not one to break. "I just worked through the tasks and did not break. I didn't realize it at first," Mike said. "But I came to understand that this was what successful mentoring involved. It accelerated my achievement."

Learn from What You See and Experience

A recent article in our local newspaper told of a situation that illustrates the strong connection that exists between the ability to learn from experiences and success in one's work. In Florence, Kentucky, a woman named Brenda Beers-Reineke walked away from her job at Swedcast

Corporation in 1977 because she was rebuffed in her efforts to land a position in customer service. Presumably, higher-ups there saw her as a secretary, which she was. What they could not see was that she had other possibilities waiting to be developed if only she were given a chance. As they saw it, Brenda did not have the background or ability to learn how to take on more challenging work. They could not get this false impression of her out of their minds. Feeling "rubbed the wrong way," Brenda walked across the street to a company called Sweco, a maker of industrial filtration equipment, where she landed a job immediately.

Wanting to go places in this company, Sweco, Brenda enrolled at a nearby college where she studied nights and on weekends to earn her bachelor's and MBA degrees. After that, she went on to earn a law degree. Starting as a secretary, Brenda learned and worked her way through Sweco's sales division. "With each year of education, Sweco always seemed to come through and offer me a new opportunity," she said. Today, Brenda Beers-Reineke is president of Sweco, a company that employs about 280 people in Florence and about 700 worldwide. Revealed in this newspaper article about Beers-Reineke is her remarkable ability to learn from her experiences, especially from what she observed firsthand. She watched what went on around her and cataloged valuable lessons and then she applied them. This ability served to move her ahead. A thirty-eight-year veteran at Sweco, Peter Knox said, "What makes her a good leader is her mixture of caring about people and their accomplishments as well as recognizing their strengths and weaknesses. She's just really good with people." Brenda said that she acquired valuable lessons in managing people from observing what went on around her, particularly while she worked as a secretary. "When I started working and climbing the ladder, people at lower levels were treated differently," she said. "There's a mutual respect, long overdue, that wasn't there. I always thought that I wanted to climb the ladder so I could treat people the way I wish I had been treated."

The story of Brenda demonstrates an important principle: we can learn from our experiences by being observant and reflecting on what we notice. One of the most limiting beliefs humans have is the notion that learning stops at the schoolhouse door. While it is true that learning occurs when a person reads or hears information given out by another person, it is also true that learning often arises through an individual's own efforts. The most mentally alive people you and I will meet are those who are extraordinarily curious and observant and whose minds are constantly in gear trying to interpret what they see. This is precisely what Brenda did—she saw how others were treated and how they reacted. By thinking about what she saw, Brenda developed definite ideas as to how people respond and perform as a result of their treatment. In so doing, she schooled herself in the basics of human relations, leadership, and motivation. She saw what it took to be an effective leader—how to excite and inspire people to high-level performance and how not to create hostility and resentment in employees.

All too often, we tend to take conventional wisdom to be the last word on things. When we do this we prevent ourselves from learning and cause our learning skills to diminish. While there is much to be said in favor of learning from the combined wisdom of the human race, there will always be found instances where conventional wisdom is just plain wrong. The history of science provides plenty of examples that illustrate the importance of independent thinking and learning through observation as opposed to taking someone else's word for the way things are. In the sixteenth century a Belgian anatomist and physician named Andreas Vesalius (1514–1564) changed medicine when he broke with tradition by dissecting human cadavers. This was one of the beginning points in experimental science and it helped usher in the Renaissance. The more bodies Vesalius dissected, the more he came to realize that earlier anatomy texts were just plain wrong—humans do not share the same anatomy as apes, as was previously believed. Vesalius produced anatomical charts of the blood and nervous system, and in 1543 he published the first modern text on the human anatomy, *On the Workings of the Human Body*. For those in medicine who came after him, the human body, directly observed, was the only reliable source.

Be Curious. Look for Opportunities to Learn

Samuel Johnson, that great English scholar and noted wit (1709–1784), captured a vital truth when he said that curiosity is a characteristic of a vigorous intellect. Curiosity prods us to admit what we don't understand, pushing us to overcome our ignorance by acquiring new knowledge. What we would otherwise allow to pass by unnoticed and leave unexamined, curiosity drives us to explore and understand. Without curiosity, it is easy to allow ourselves to drift into the sleep of complacency. The way to a fuller, more exciting, and more richly rewarding existence demands a healthy level of curiosity.

Be curious! This is exactly what Douglas Danforth, former chairman and CEO of Westinghouse, urged young men and women who worked in his organization to do. "Have curiosity about what's around you," he told them. "In the business world, if you start out in engineering, have a curiosity about marketing, about manufacturing, about finance. Don't let yourself stay just within your own envelope or your own discipline. Because people are very willing to share their knowledge and experience, the most flattering thing you can do is to ask them, 'Tell me a little about what you do in marketing. I don't understand anything about it. Would you mind having lunch with me, or if I stopped by after work, would you chat with me? Could I make a trip when you go to call on a customer? I've never sold anything.'"

When he was a young man starting out in his career, this is what Danforth himself did. Because he was curious, he asked questions, lots of questions. He learned from the answers he received, and because of that, he grew. He began his career in manufacturing. But when he looked out upon his company he saw a broad vista of learning opportunities. He wanted to know more about these other areas. Marketing and finance aroused his interest. The more he learned, the more he saw there was to learn. Demonstrating a bit of curiosity served him well, and he moved from one job to another, all the way to the very top of his company.

It's impossible to be curious unless you are humble. Socrates opened many a pair of eyes to what humility involves when he said, "I neither know nor think that I know." The important lesson to be grasped here is this: it is humility that allows people to recognize their ignorance. Once humility is reached, curiosity can arise and lead to improvement. The capacity to wonder is at the heart of curiosity. Imagine a small child on a summer's day, lying on the ground watching ants scurrying about, toting what appear to be tremendous loads in comparison to their tiny bodies. Curiosity involves looking at things and asking oneself questions: "What makes it work? How does it happen?" But these are only a start.

Keep Your Mind Active and Growing Stronger

The human brain can continue to increase its powers of thoughtful analysis and imagination far into later life. Continued development depends on how one chooses to use and exercise this magnificent gift. Our mental powers and spiritual qualities are perfected through constant use, especially when they are challenged to work hard. But let the mind rest too long, remove all challenge and novel experience, and it will grow weak and flaccid. As with body muscles, the mind will waste away if not exercised regularly. Do the same things day after day, don't experience new challenges, remove the possibility of challenge, and limit what you read or see and the people you encounter—this is the perfect prescription for rigidity and narrowness of thought, a sure and quick route to obsolescence.

It has been said that one of life's great tragedies occurs when a person's mind dies while the rest of the body lives on. Over time, as we've all seen, many people lose their enthusiasm for living. They grow cynical about the future. Their mental alertness declines. Their zest for enjoying good things dwindles. Their inclination and ability to notice beauty and things meaningful and humorous grind to a halt. They become unable and unwilling to savor the moment. We are all vulnerable to these sad endings. Unwanted and unnoticed forces assault us daily, pushing us toward mental stagnation and its evil cousin, cynicism. These forces include: unthinking habit, fear of failure, doing just enough to get by, procrastination, overreliance on old solutions and methods, avoidance of opportunities and fear of challenging endeavors because they seem too complex or difficult, unchanging routine void of new experience, and the attitude, "I already know enough to get by." The mind is a wonderful gift, intended for you to use and develop all your life.

MASTER THE ART
OF SELF-DISCIPLINE

Assess Your Actions Honestly, Cause Your Emotions to Work for You, Learn to Make Favorable Impressions

"To be human is to be self-conscious; and to be self-conscious is to bring one's self into the sphere of art, as an object to be judged, altered, improved."

William Ernest Hocking

You can become a very great asset to yourself by mastering the art of self-discipline. This begins with the habit of inspecting your actions or inactions and identifying where they measure up to what you want them to be or fall short of ideals. The art of self-discipline also involves accepting the reality of your primitive instincts and setting them to useful purposes. Imagine what life might be like if humans didn't have the capacity to inspect and correct their own behavior. Civilization would be impossible. Simply put, we would be unable to get along with others. Self-discipline enables humans to be punctual, to act with perseverance, to be industrious, to rise above pettiness, to focus efforts on important matters and produce desired results. No good life has yet been lived without a goodly amount of self-discipline.

The recipe for self-discipline involves two ingredients—self-inspection and habit-building. Every school kid remembers reading about Ben Franklin, that wise old American patriot who gave us bifocals, the Franklin stove, and the knowledge that lightning was electricity. Ben knew that unwanted defects in our character have a way, over time, of becoming more ingrained and increasingly difficult to change. He devised a method to dislodge unwanted personal habits. It was a simple method to perfect himself. Every day he would evaluate his own behavior against a list of virtues, marking a grade for himself as a teacher would do for her students. This practice of self-examination produced admirable habits in Ben and enabled him to live an extraordinary life. "Habits are acquired by acting," says William J. Byron, S.J., "You have to do—now and repeatedly—that which you want eventually to do easily and habitually."

Learn to Defeat the Procrastination Urge

Procrastination. It's putting off doing what ought to be done—like writing bills, taking out the garbage, fixing that broken latch on the screen door, disciplining a badly performing employee, quitting a bad job, asking for a raise. We know of a want-to-be artist who craves for the day to come when she will muster enough courage to say "yes" to her dream of traveling the country where she can paint landscapes. Unfortunately, she continues to put *that day* off, making it *tomorrow* instead of *today*. "There are just too many demands being made on me now," she tells her friends. "I'll do it when I have more time." The years have a way of rolling by. And they do just that. Meanwhile, she continues to put her dreams on hold, thinking to herself, "I'll pursue my painting plans some day, but not right now."

We have all heard more than once the old adage that a dose of humility is good for the soul. Humility allows us to be human and to see more deeply into ourselves. I (Charles) find that humility opens our minds to ideas that will lead us to be better persons. So here and now I have a confession to make. All afternoon today and before getting down to the business of writing I have been putting off writing this chapter on self-control. I admit it. I procrastinated! Let's consider the reasons behind the urge to procrastinate.

It's astounding to see the number and variety of little things that a person will find time to do to avoid doing what's most important. As I am now just sitting down at my computer to begin this chapter it is twenty minutes past four in the afternoon. Up until now I have avoided writing because I didn't know exactly what to say and how to say it. This was uncomfortable and I didn't want to face the difficult job of having to think. So, ever since finishing my lunch, I avoided writing. I did that by finding other things to do. I sat and read for a half hour and looked at the notes that I have been keeping on ideas for this chapter. I got bored with that and felt sleepy, so I took a nap. Sleep generally affords us a fairly effective escape—but it is only a temporary escape. I awoke and realized that I must get back to work. Oh, how I wanted to avoid that! I delayed thinking and writing some more. I went outside and checked to see what had come in the mail. Then I did a load of laundry. While my washing machine worked I went into another room where it was quiet and I phoned my brother in California. We talked about last summer's fishing trip in Idaho and his high school daughter's first volleyball game of the season. We talked about where we might fish next summer. He had to get back to work, and my escape from what I should be doing ended. I found another way of avoiding the dreaded writing that hung over my head: I telephoned a painter and talked with him about a job and scheduled a time for him to stop by and survey the work to be done.

Knowing that I was not getting a single word written gnawed away at me. Nothing could rid my mind and heart of the uncomfortable feeling that came from knowing progress was not being made on something I felt should be done. Regardless, I continued to procrastinate. What else could I do instead of working on this chapter? I built a tiller for a friend's sailboat yesterday. So, to keep myself busy and avoid writing a bit longer, I spent the past thirty minutes sanding it and applying a first coat of varnish. Then, an idea hit me, as if it were a gift from the Almighty. While I worked on the tiller something dawned on me: "Here I am trying to decide how to explain the difficulty we all face called procrastination. I knew that I was doing this very thing myself. Why not admit it and write about this experience? After all, we all go through it. It seems to be a superb idea. Just maybe in doing that, I could delve more deeply into the reasons why people procrastinate."

What I came to realize from examining my own predicament this afternoon is this: procrastination results very often from not knowing what to do and how to proceed. It comes when we face complicated tasks that we don't know where or how to begin. Instead, we do other things to make us feel that we are not altogether lazy and worthless.

An excellent way for anyone to get up the strength needed to defeat the procrastination urge is to admit it whenever it is working against you. You will be stronger and emotionally better off whenever you look at yourself squarely and admit what you are doing. Admit it when you are putting off doing what you know you should be doing. Examples aplenty, however, demonstrate that this suggestion is not as easy to follow as one might think. Humans develop all sorts of mind-satisfying excuses that hold them in the trap of procrastination.

One of these excuses is that they look at what ought to be done as being too trivial to bother with right now. Enabled by what might be called the "I'm above it" attitude, many people damage themselves through their procrastination. A highly educated woman, a college professor we know, put off paying a traffic citation. After getting several notices reminding her of her obligation, she received a summons to appear in court and explain why she failed to pay the fine. The letter from the court stated in no uncertain terms that failure to appear would result in an arrest warrant. That got her attention. Now she had to cancel a scheduled class examination, which necessitated informing her department chair and her students. The students were annoyed at having to adjust their schedules and her department chair's opinion of her diminished. Unneeded expense, trouble, anxiety, and resentment came as a consequence of her procrastination.

Beyond the immediate effects of not getting work done on time, failure to control the procrastination urge invites long-term damage to individuals themselves. Procrastination weakens one's ability and will to improve oneself and to eliminate undesirable habits. Over time undesirable habits usually grow until they become insurmountable. No one may be harmed by neglecting to do small tasks, but prolonged delays in developing responsible and productive habits destroy the possibility of improvement.

It is important to recognize that procrastination occurs whenever a person thinks an action or a change in behavior will be too difficult or too uncomfortable to bear. You can be certain that procrastination is doing its dirty work whenever you hear remarks like these: "I'm afraid to schedule an appointment for a medical test, because I fear the doctors might detect I have a dreaded disease." "I'm not going to make that phone call to the upset customer because I don't feel like being bawled out." "I don't want to start on the job of improving our company's information needs assessment right now because it will be too difficult to figure out." These are things most people would just as soon avoid doing, so they procrastinate.

One good way to escape the clutches of procrastination is to ask yourself the right question. Effective performers do not ask, "Can I afford the difficulties that change requires?" but, instead, "Can I afford the consequences of not changing?" They seize the initiative without hesitation. They act while it is still day, before it is too late. An important benefit that comes from getting something done right away is the psychological lift that comes from knowing that the unpleasant task is out of the way—or, at least the difficult first step has begun—and you can relax a bit in just knowing that. When I was in high school a friend once said to me, "You sleep better when you've completed your homework and you know that you don't have it hanging over your head to do the next morning." I don't have any scientific proof of this but from my experience, I think he was right.

Direct Your "Inner Caveman" toward Useful Ends

A rudimentary fact of life is that destructive tendencies are to be found within every human being no matter how well-meaning and disciplined that person is. The exterior is usually one of outward respectability, guided by reason and civility. But inside, humans are plagued with impulses—lustful, angry, hurtful. Our nature has a disturbing duality to it much like that depicted in Robert Louis Stevenson's *Dr. Jekyll and Mr. Hyde*. It is very important to deal with ourselves as we really are, not as we might prefer to think of ourselves. Those who succeed in life do more than *not* allowing their base desires and primitive instincts to crowd out their finer desires. They know how to channel their primitive instincts into higher purposes.

One practical difficulty everyone faces is that of living with their lowest instincts and primitive desires. High ideals and civility resonate positively with people's saintly side. Their minds nod acceptance to those virtues that civilization honors: humility, kindness, decency, fairness, to name a few. These are the ideals that caring people try to cultivate within themselves and project outward for others to see. They try hard to be high-minded, principled, controlled. They try to guide their behavior by reason and love. But life is never simple and it cannot be shielded from ugly realities. Temptations are inevitable. Tempers can run hot and flare out of control. Some problems frustrate our efforts and others cause us grief. Selfish desires have a way of seducing the highest of the high-minded, while ambitions and wants cry out to be fulfilled and satisfied. Our minds are quick to see where unlovely or uncaring actions might secure a desired gain or defeat a rival.

Conflicts and annoyances are found in every workplace, especially those in which there are people with different outlooks, values, and agendas from our own. We should ask ourselves: What should we do when we are annoyed or angered by a workplace condition or an action by another person? Our high-minded, idealistic side wants us to take "the high road," not to allow our emotions to lead us to do things for which we would feel sorry later on. But our darker instincts—those coming from our inner caveman—urge us to respond in cruder and more forceful ways. Just think of the many conflicts that arise between what our high-mindedness tells us is smart and what our primitive instincts urge us to do.

- A woman we know named Amanda turned in a piece of work recently that her boss saw as "unacceptable." The boss came down hard on Amanda, telling Amanda that she was not pleased. Amada felt that her boss saw her as being stupid and lazy and indifferent to her unit's performance. Hurt and embarrassed, Amanda first grew angry, then began to long to get even with her boss.
- During the annual planning session, the people in Walter's sales division discussed new methods for meeting next year's targets. Unfortunately, Walter viewed these ideas not as suggestions but as challenges to his opinions. Walter lost his self-control. Outraged, he argued against their ideas with considerable sarcasm.
- Gloria feels that her company owes her more than she is getting paid. She is tempted to run errands during working hours. She uses the telephone for personal calls, she takes time off for personal reasons, and she pads her expense account.

Our minds know that bad behavior arising out of anger and irritation is usually self-defeating. We know that the abrasive person is shunned, the egoistic coworker is ridiculed, and the hurtful person is dealt meanness in return. We know that one never fully "wins" by using the methods and actions our inner caveman wants us to adopt. Yet these bad behaviors have a way of erupting anyway. When they do, our idealistic side puts our inner caveman on trial for having caused them. And a "Guilty!" verdict is rendered almost immediately. Our barbarian within becomes penitent. But this remorse is never permanent. Trouble still lurks beneath the surface.

You might try to control your inner-caveman instincts by telling yourself the same things adults told you when you were a youngster: "Behave yourself, control your temper." "Do not give in to your unwholesome desires." These words of advice might sound logical, and they usually work. At least they do for a while. We follow the conventional wisdom to restrain our base urges—we try chaining them down, so as to not give in to their demands. But this self-imposed restraint is never a fully workable solution, because we are human. In time the vile and uncivil barbarian within will escape and there will be hell to pay. Uncontrolled emotions, uncivil words, excessive pride expressed through self-flattery, downright mean actions, and overambition that stops at nothing—these are some of the many ways the inner caveman turns good persons into dreaded terrors. And so a war rages on within each normal human. The finer desires and higher ideals we would like to live by are pitted against the inner-caveman instincts of our native makeup. We need to find a way out of the disunited state in which we find ourselves.

It is very important in life to recognize what we can and what we cannot do. If we give free rein to our low desires we find that they eventually bring about unwelcome consequences. If we try to crush them or chain them to a prison wall, we find that they escape and cause mischief. But there is another way of dealing with this dilemma.

Over many millennia humans have developed certain native capacities necessary to their survival. Self-preservation, egoism, pugnacity, anger—these are useful drives and instincts that serve us well if directed with laser-like precision. History reveals that the best lives have not always been those which have succeeded in eliminating these low desires. Instead, they are lives that have learned how to harness dangerous, natural instincts and direct them to useful purposes. Think of it: egotism can be useful in pursuing superlative quality and ongoing improvement. Combativeness can be a useful ally in breaking down barriers of racial prejudice or making needed changes in an organization's direction. Outspoken bluntness can be put to use in calling bad practices what they really are and unmasking those who are more fluff than substance.

To live successfully with one's inner-caveman instincts it's always advisable to catalog what they are and to identify the specific circumstances when they will most likely appear. One person we know extremely well recognizes his intolerance for bureaucratic red tape and excessive governmental regulations. Having to negotiate his way through massive amounts of regulatory details usually elicits a tone of nasty sarcasm from him and leads him to become combative. To his credit, this person wisely chooses to stay away from situations that might cause him annoyance. Once, for instance, he got someone else who is untroubled by local building requirements and permit-granting processes to handle the job of securing approval from a historical preservation agency for a building project. Realizing that he might get angry, he chose to stay away from this small-yet-important aspect of the project. Instead, he used his impatient nature to push ahead with other business that needed to be done.

Rise Above the Tendency to Envy Others

We once met a man from Chicago who headed the National Can Company at the time. Frank Considine had risen through the ranks all the way to the very top of his organization, where he was chairman and CEO. Few people get this far in their careers. Some of the things that he revealed about himself helped us understand an important factor behind his success. Frank told us that when he was a year into his first job with National Can, another man worked alongside of him doing essentially the same job—selling cans. Frank was selling more product than this other man and the other man didn't like it. So, naturally, the other man began to envy Frank's success.

At first the man's envy led to nothing more than a friendly rivalry. But after a time, and with Frank outselling all the others in his unit, this other man's ego got rubbed raw and he started taking it out on Frank. The two men, who had started out being friends, were fast becoming enemies. Frank considered what was happening and he decided that it was not good for him to respond to this other man's nastiness and underhanded remarks. It wasn't good, Frank thought, for his company. And it wasn't good for this other man either. So Frank decided to not respond to the bad things the other man said about him or did. Frank just kept trying to be friends with him and to prevent animosity from ruining what had once been a pretty good friendship. After several years the other man realized that Frank really wasn't his enemy. In fact his real enemy was within himself—it was his less-than-stellar selling skills, which were not all that bad. In fact the other man was a darn good salesman; he just wasn't the best salesman. After realizing what was going on in his mind, this other man went to Frank and admitted he was wrong to be jealous and envious. This action sort of cleared the air and the two men became friends once more. They remained friends ever since.

Humankind has long known the destructive possibilities of envy. The ancient Israelites were instructed by God, in the Ten Commandments, not to covet their neighbor's belongings or his wife or servants. For a person wanting to find ways to be envious of others the opportunities are endless. There is always some other person who has better looks, more imagination, superior skills, more money, finer collections. Envy arises from a sense of one's deficiencies, limits, failures. Thus, in truth, envy is the experience of hating oneself for being less than someone else—less wealthy, less beautiful, less skillful, et cetera. If you can learn to avoid envy you will save yourself from a great deal of self-inflicted misery.

Whenever you find that another person has what you want to possess, the possibility of envy is not far away. The threat envy poses to ourselves lies not merely in feeling jealous of others but in allowing our envy to grow out of control and become all-consuming. In a sense, envy can "eat us alive." It eats away at the qualities that make people likeable. It stops them from being the persons that they were uniquely created to be. You can see this going on around you whenever you notice neighbors trying to keep up with those around them—building bigger homes, buying more expensive automobiles, sending their children off to more prestigious schools, acquiring a summer house in an expensive resort area. Envy can even lead us into being nasty, bitter people who are so deeply consumed with wanting what others have that we are unable to do well with our own unique talents. It can even prevent us from ever accomplishing those purposes that we are best suited to achieve. Envy can grow large and become all-consuming. It has caused some individuals to do terrible things. A story appeared in the morning sports pages recently that illustrates the power envy can have over a person. In Greeley, Colorado, the University of Northern Colorado's reserve punter was arrested, accused of stabbing his rival in the kicking leg. Three men had been in competition for the starting punter's job in preseason training and the coach had settled on who he wanted in the punter's position. The starting punter had performed well, averaging over thirty-seven yards per punt on nine punts in two games. So, one night, in a parking lot, the reserve punter allegedly stabbed the starter in the leg.

What can one do to combat envy? The first thing to do is to recognize it for what it is. Envy is a common human emotion. We all experience it. A useful first step to help yourself rise above envy is to recognize it happening whenever it shows itself in your heart. Go ahead and admit when you are envious of others and examine the reasons behind your envy. "What exactly is it that you are envious of?" This simple acknowledgement allows a person to feel "one" with every other human being on earth in that the feeling is a normal human response to situations when one realizes others have more or are seemingly better off.

If you think about it carefully, you'll find that you are not envious of your friends and loved ones when you are feeling good and confident about yourself and your life. We are only envious when we feel low, inadequate, or missing something in our lives. It is when we are in a negative state of mind, made so by worry about ourselves or feeling annoyed that others appear better off than we are, that envy attacks us. How then can you put yourself in a positive state where envy cannot raise its ugly head and attack you? The answer many successful people tell us is this: Get busy with a duty to fulfill, a cause to serve, an adventure to take. When our feelings are strong and aimed in exciting directions, we are not open to the invitations of envy.

Another useful method of dealing with envy involves developing wisdom. We see things and we wish we could possess them ourselves; we envy those who have them. But if we are wise we will ask ourselves these questions: "Are these things really all that important to me? Will having them make me any more content than I am or any more the person I would like to become and feel comfortable being? Are these things really of as great worth as I perceive them to be?" Are we really capable of telling whether the thing we look at is worth envying? Many times, in retrospect, people find that when they do get what they thought they wanted, they are no happier, no better off, no more fulfilled or self-confident than they were beforehand. In wisdom they oftentimes find that what they thought they wanted was not worth valuing or envying at all.

You can escape the self-defeating forces of envy by developing within yourself the tendency to focus your thoughts on doing positive things instead of merely acquiring things. The trick is to find projects and purposes suitable to your talents and passions and then busying yourself with achieving them. The more you do this the more you will accomplish and the more lasting satisfaction you'll experience.

Improve Your Productivity!

Countless performance shortcomings haunt the workplaces around the world because people haven't developed the self-discipline to search out better methods and be more productive: a salesperson continues to follow outdated and ineffective methods; a clerk fails to do a better job of greeting customers and creating in them a mood to buy; a delivery truck driver fails to record important information that others need in order to track shipments. The next time you walk past the places where people are working, notice what they are doing. It may surprise you to find some who seem very comfortable doing nothing, or very little at best. Once, in 1973, when I (Charles) had an appointment at the Social Security Administration I discovered something astounding. The headquarters building, on Social Security Way in Baltimore, Maryland, is huge. It must cover many acres and employ hundreds of people. As I wound my way down one hallway and then another that morning, I passed by dozens of offices and could not help but notice those inside. They were talking on the telephone, reading newspapers, talking to others, drinking coffee. But what surprised me was that not one person I saw that morning—and I passed by dozens of offices filled with people—appeared to be working.

What modern technology has blessed us with it has, at the same time, cursed us with. Take the computer, that marvelous information-processing instrument and our connector to the information highway. Is it a help or a distraction? If you walk by the desks where people are supposed to be getting important things done, you will find many playing card games on their computers. The Internet provides access to an endless number of Web sites containing more information and entertainment than we can possibly read in a lifetime. While we can benefit from selective usage of this window on the world, the Internet, we should be aware of the possibility that we can become addicted to visiting it to the detriment of our productivity. We can allow the Internet to steal our time and misuse our talents.

A surprisingly large number of capable people make themselves less effective than they could be not because they don't do anything but because they expend their efforts on matters of little consequence. A designer named Audrey we learned about recently once promised to have a proposal ready for a potential client late one week. The client scheduled an appointment at three o'clock on a Friday afternoon to hear Audrey's ideas. The possibility of landing a big contract was attractive. Audrey fully intended to be ready for the presentation but when the hour neared she found herself far from being prepared. Time seemed to pass by more quickly than she imagined it would and, like a school kid unprepared for a spelling test, Audrey panicked, but only at the last minute. How did Audrey get herself into this predicament?

In the days preceding the scheduled appointment a series of unexpected interruptions cropped up, and Audrey yielded to them. They literally stole her time and kept her from preparing for her scheduled presentation. There were phone calls, small problems, interruptions, and an unexpected luncheon invitation—all the kinds of things that eat into a person's time. At 1:30 in the afternoon on the day of the scheduled appointment, Audrey lifted her telephone receiver to call the client. Knowing that it would be impossible to have a suitable presentation by 3:00 that afternoon, she searched her mind for an excuse. What could she tell her client? Her thoughts raced through one possible excuse after another. Audrey's problem wasn't that she was lazy, her problem was that she didn't have the self-discipline to keep her efforts focused where they would make the biggest impact.

Many years ago a business professor named Tom McNichols from Northwestern University wrote a case study that captured the essence of the tendency that plagued Audrey. "The Case of the Missing Time" that McNichols penned has provided students of time management with one of the best real-world descriptions of how time can slip away. This case is a "must read" for anyone who is interested in developing the knowledge and willpower needed to take control of one's time. The case tells of one day in the life of a man named Chet Craig who manages a printing plant. During his morning drive to work Chet reviews in his mind all the things he hopes to accomplish that day and places priorities on them. Number one on his list is the establishment of a new scheduling procedure to improve productivity dramatically and save on costs and reduce delays in finished work shipments. But Chet never gets around to this task. From the time he enters the plant gates till the time he leaves work for his drive home, Chet is confronted with one request or problem to solve after another—and those who study the case become tired just reading of all the minutiae that gobble up Chet's time. He has to find a replacement for a new hire. He's asked to decide what to do with slow-moving stock. An underling demands a solution to a packing problem. Chet visits the plant floor and hears complaints from employees working there. He reschedules vacation times. The list is long and confusing and tiring to read. At the end of the day Chet is exhausted and not one step closer to completing what he wanted to complete, what he believes is most important to accomplish.

What can we do to escape our tendency to do little things while big ones go undone? There is a very old story and no one alive today can say for sure whether it is 100 percent true, but it's worth retelling here because its message is enormously valuable. A consultant named Ivy Lee whose clients included many of the giants of American enterprise of the previous century—Rockefeller, Morgan, the DuPonts, to name a few—once called on Charles Schwab, president of Bethlehem Steel. As Ivy Lee outlined all the expertise he could provide Bethlehem Steel, he told Schwab that, "With our services you'll know how to manage better."

Schwab was a man of action. He was also skeptical of the smooth-talking Lee. "We don't need more knowing," Schwab told Ivy Lee. "What we need is more doing!" He went on to tell Lee that Bethlehem Steel would gladly pay him anything reasonable if he could get employees actually to do all the things that they already knew they ought to do. Lee thought a moment about what he just heard. "Fine," he told Schwab. "If you'll give me just 20 minutes, I will explain how you can improve efficiency here by at least 50%." Realizing that he had about half an hour before he had to leave to catch a train, Schwab told Lee to go ahead and present his idea. Here is the idea that Ivy Lee explained to Schwab.

Lee produced an index card from his pocket and gave it to Schwab. "Write on this card the six most important things you have to do tomorrow," said Lee. Schwab took the card, thought and wrote down his top six priorities. This took him about three minutes. "Now," said Lee, "number these in order of their importance." Schwab thought and considered each priority carefully. Five more minutes passed as Schwab thought and numbered each item listed. "Okay, now keep this card in your coat pocket and when you begin work tomorrow pull it out and start working on item #1. Pull the card out of your pocket every 15 minutes throughout the day and keep working at #1 until it is finished. Then tackle #2 in the same way; then item #3. Do this until quitting time. Don't be concerned if you only finish one item. The others can wait. You'll be working on what's more important. If you cannot finish them by this method, you couldn't finish them by any other method either. And, without some system, you'd probably not even decide which are the most important. Spend the last five minutes of every day making a 'Must Do List' for the next day. After you've convinced yourself of the worth of this idea, have your people try it. Use this method consciously as long as you wish and then send me a check for what you think it is worth." The entire interview lasted about twenty-five minutes.

In two weeks Schwab sent Lee a check for $25,000—about a thousand dollars a minute that Lee spent with Schwab. Schwab added a note saying Lee's lesson was the most profitable advice he ever took.

Learn How to Make Favorable Impressions

Let's face it. We all want others to think of us as being competent, intelligent, cooperative, and congenial. We want them to regard us highly. Have you ever considered how your behavior influences the way others regard you? It has been demonstrated countless times that first impressions have more to do with how a person is regarded than practically anything else. For one thing, first impressions have a way of sticking. Once another person begins to gather and process basic information about us, we create an image of ourselves in their minds and it tends to remain there, intact, for a long while. It is important to remember that others take in a very small sample of us before they make up their minds about us. This may not be logical or fair. Nonetheless, that's the way it is. It therefore becomes critically important to know how to make the right impressions.

Many people doom themselves to failure by making a bad impression. A friend of ours named Gail once ran a temporary employment agency. Her job involved finding qualified people to send out to area employers for temporary work assignments. Naturally, it was critically important to the success of Gail's company to send out only those people who would perform effectively. A woman once came to Gail's firm for an interview. Trying to make a good impression, this woman wanted to be seen as alive and open. Unfortunately, she was too alive, too open. Once she began speaking she didn't stop. She told Gail of her divorce, her children, her last place of employment and the work she did there. She talked about those with whom she had last worked and why she liked some and disliked others. She discussed her drive to the interview. She had a strong opinion about the weather, and about the road conditions she encountered. She told of her friends and the troubles they were having with husbands and boyfriends. She brought up her last doctor's visit, her ailments, and the medicines she was taking. Gail sat there and wondered to herself, *What's with this woman?* She did not stop talking for even a brief moment but went on and on. Before long the woman's unstoppable talking became annoying. Gail realized that if this woman's constant talking began to bother her after only ten minutes it would surely irritate others in the workplace working alongside this woman day after day. Her constant talking would do her in.

When meeting someone for the first time, you might feel that making a favorable impression involves doing things that will cause the other person to think well of you. Your instincts will probably tell you to "sell yourself." If you follow this urge, you will likely concentrate on yourself, on your behavior. You will try to project your "best." You will try to act in ways to make yourself look good. If you want to make a good impression, this is exactly the wrong focus to take. Here's why. Those who are most successful in making favorable impressions know that it's not how they come across that counts so much as it is how they make others feel about themselves in their presence. Does the other person feel appreciated, elevated, enlightened, and connected through some commonly held interest or experience? If you act in a way that makes the other person feel understood and happy, they will likely project these feelings onto you.

Check yourself: Do you act in ways that cause others to feel insulted, alienated, unappealing? If so, then you can be sure that they will not have a good feeling about you. If you annoy them by trying too hard to be seen as funny, or if you laugh at everything you say, your actions will drive them away. Crude remarks, condescending comments, inappropriate disclosures—these also tend to push others off. Highly effective people show a sincere interest in others. They recognize them as human beings with feelings and abilities worth knowing. They connect with others by finding some common ground, some interest or experience they might share. They say things that elevate and encourage the other person in something they do or want to do. They enlighten the other person with an interesting bit of information—without being boring or acting as a know-it-all.

People who fail in life are often those who cannot control their tongues. You know the type: they are overly quick to criticize others, offer their evaluations of what's going on, they try to be funny and say things that aren't funny, or they jump to conclusions and voice them before all the information available is known. It takes a very wise person to have enough sense to keep quiet and say nothing when doing just the opposite is so tempting. Many individuals have done themselves serious and lasting harm because they spoke too soon, before they thought out what they were about to say, and uttered words that they wished they had never voiced. Sometimes what comes out of a person's mouth is offensive even though the person making the offensive remark was merely trying to be funny and really didn't mean it at all. Regardless, after it comes out, it's too late to retract it. The damage has been done.

We all prefer to do business with people who display good manners and are principled in the practices of fair play and friendly competition. Manners have an untold impact on creating goodwill and positive impressions. I (Charles) heard once about a salesperson named Dan who was invited by a designer to prepare a proposal to a client. This client would then choose between several competitors who were also making proposals for the same job. The invitation came by way of a designer who recommended several providers. When it was announced that a rival had "won" the contract, the salesperson, Dan, wrote a short note of thanks to the designer for arranging the opportunity to compete. Whom do you suppose the designer will have on his list for the next client to consider? You can choose to be an appreciative competitor or a person who sulks and becomes angry because his products were not chosen.

Develop the Punctuality Advantage

A woman we know in her twenties, highly talented and well-educated, made an appointment for a job interview in San Francisco at a top-notch graphic design studio a few years back. Apparently the importance of the scheduled time meant little to her. Portfolio in hand, she arrived nearly two hours late. Although they went ahead and interviewed her, the prospective employer wasn't impressed. It wasn't that this young woman didn't have the talent to do the work. It was that her lateness demonstrated an unwillingness to abide by schedules, something that is a vital element for running a business effectively.

Punctuality shows what we think about others, how much we respect them and their time. We recently came across an article that argued people arrive late to appointments because they feel the other person might be late and they don't want to be kept waiting themselves. This might be true with some people. But what does it say about them? We think it says, "I don't care if you have to wait. Just don't make me wait." Sounds pretty selfish, doesn't it? It is!

Several years ago I (Charles) scheduled a morning meeting with a man named John Folkerth, president of Shopsmith, Inc. in Dayton, Ohio. His company manufactures and markets a line of power tools. After arriving and sitting down in his office Folkerth quite deliberately looked at his wrist watch and asked me, "What time did you think this appointment was for?" I said, "Nine o'clock." Folkerth told me, "I have it on my calendar for 8 A.M." Although he was not subtle in letting me know that I was an hour late, he was effective in communicating the importance he placed on time and being punctual. Actually, he was right about the scheduled time. I had, somehow, gotten the time of our appointment wrong in my mind. The point of this story is that successful people place a high value on time and have the habit of being punctual.

Being late to everything is a sign of disorganization. If this sounds like you, don't despair—at least just yet. It is a "fixable" flaw. There are several practical things anyone can do to correct perpetual lateness: (1) Get into the right mind-set. Resolve to be on time to all appointments, especially your next one. Make a commitment to yourself that you will be punctual. (2) Make a note of when you must be somewhere and the time you must leave from where you start out so that you will have plenty of time to arrive there without having to hurry. (3) Set your times so that you have an extra five to ten minutes to spare and have something with you so that when you do arrive early you have something productive to do, like reading notes or letters. (4) Always allow more time than you think necessary for driving, finding a parking space, and so on. (5) Refuse to allow some last-minute "emergency" to stop you from leaving on time. (6) Finally, just moments before you have to leave, don't get diverted from a timely departure by allowing yourself to try to finish one last thing, one more task, or change into other clothing just because it is not entirely, 100 percent "right."

Know What Your Appearance Says to Others

Through a recent experience I (Charles) was reminded of the importance of personal hygiene and good grooming. It happened a few months ago when I was checking out at my local grocery store. The clerk behind the cash register looked unkempt. He had a three-day stubble of whiskers. He wore a dirty shirt. He had facial piercing and tattoos up and down his arms. As I watched him handle my groceries— bread, milk, fruit, meat—I felt sick. Here was this dirty man handling the food that I would be taking home to prepare and eat.

It may be flatly stated that appearance matters. It matters to those who decide who gets hired. It matters to those who decide who gets promoted. It matters to those who decide who gets placed in plum positions. And it matters to customers and any of the public with whom employees come into contact. A good appearance sends positive signals; a bad appearance sends negative signals. Our first line of communication we have with others is our appearance. It's our dress, our grooming, and our posture. In the work setting we signal what we think of ourselves, how much we respect our organization, and what we would like others to think of us, by our appearance. I (Tom) remember the time when, at thirteen years old, I got a minimum-wage job working at a fruit stand in Portland, Oregon. I remember my mother insisting that I wear a clean white shirt and have my hair combed. She said, "When you are working there remember that you are representing your boss. You want to make a good impression with the public."

An important distinction to keep in mind is that appearance is not the same thing as beauty. Few people have sexy bodies. Few can afford expensive cosmetics and glamorous clothes and accessories. Appearance means grooming, first and foremost. It also means posture and manners and adherence to the standards of etiquette. It involves having one's hair combed, fingernails cleaned, hands washed, clothes pressed, and shirt-tails tucked in. An ideal to strive for is to appear as if you are recently bathed, dressed, and smelling pleasant.

Good appearance is as important as good job performance. I (Tom) have been a member of my local YMCA for many years. I remember a young woman who served as a lifeguard there. She had a pleasant disposition and read serious books while watching for those swimming in the pool. But she also had a problem and it was a serious one—she stank. Her body, always in a bathing suit, gave off such an odor that one wondered how many days she had gone without bathing. She was oblivious of her appearance to others. Perhaps she just didn't care. After many complaints from patrons and repeated warnings from her supervisor, the Y's manager replaced her.

Behaviors and manners that are acceptable in some circumstances might not be acceptable at other places and situations. We were once present when a university president was seated at the head table at a banquet. One would expect flawless table manners from a person at this level of responsibility and prestige. But this university president sat, eating and talking to those around him, drinking beer right out of the bottle. At another time, we were in the audience when a group of outside consultants were making a formal presentation. Each of the invited consultants knew what he or she wanted to say and had well-prepared overheads to get their ideas across. But each one made the mistake of carrying a canned soft drink with them as they stood before their audience. And each one stopped periodically and sipped their drinks in between their lines as they spoke to their listeners. Their boorish manners spoiled their image and made their message less credible.

All too frequently, in public places, people demonstrate that they either never learned good manners or that they just don't care. If you would like to make a positive impression on those persons who occupy high-level positions in organizations, you will find the following suggestions helpful.

Appearance

- Be concerned about your appearance; take it seriously.
- Dress appropriately for your work. If you need to wear a uniform where you work, find out if you are allowed to adorn the uniform with a piece of jewelry and if so, what kind.
- Choose clothes tastefully. Wear what will compliment your body, not reveal its unappealing aspects. Wear what's appropriate for the occasion or event.

- Body piercing and tattoos and hair dyed bright unnatural colors—blue, orange, pink, green—may appeal to your sense of individuality. That's your view. Others will have their views too, and what you like they might not like. Keep in mind the standards and tastes of those whose opinions you need to win over if you want to get ahead.
- Remove your hat when you are inside a building.

In Restaurants

- Don't wear ball caps while you are seated or eating.
- Suppose you have food in your mouth and you find it necessary to get up and walk to another place in the room, perhaps to get another napkin. Remain seated and finish chewing what you have in your mouth before getting up. It is unsightly, sickening actually, to see someone walking around chewing food.
- When seated in a booth or at a table, sit up straight, don't slouch.
- Holding a fork as one would grasp a hammer makes a poor impression—it is just plain crude. Learn to hold your fork between your thumb and forefingers.
- If you are a man and a woman comes to your table, stand up.

In Public

- It may be tempting to talk on your cell phone while in public. If absolutely necessary do it discreetly and quietly or don't do it at all.
- Being loud and unruly anywhere, especially in restaurants or other public places, is flat out rude too.
- If you must chew gum, do it discreetly—better yet, don't do it in public at all.
- Be courteous to others—say, "Excuse me," when you bump into or need to get past someone or have to walk between people who are talking.
- Introduce people to each other if you know they have never met before.
- Don't swear or use crude language or make suggestive remarks.
- If you are a man and you are talking with a woman, look her in the eye. Don't stare at her chest.

Using the Telephone

- Answer the phone by announcing who you are—"Hello, This is Phil Cottell, Accounting Department."

- When you call someone and you don't know who has answered the phone, announce who you are. Don't ask, "Who is this?" (Remember, you are the one who called.)
- Speak directly into the receiver in a clear voice and don't mumble or talk too fast.

In Meetings

- Say what you need to say clearly and directly. Get to your point.
- If you express a point of view that differs from what others think or have said, be courteous. Say, "I see things differently or in a different way because." Then state your reason. Refrain from name-calling or belittling remarks.
- Be civil. Treat others with respect.

ACT WITH INTEGRITY

Know Good from Evil, Right from Wrong, Defeat Self-Centeredness, Pursue the Good and Right Wholeheartedly

"Man is a creature who can ask of an action, not merely 'Will it be praised?' but 'Ought it be?' and no amount of affirmative answers to the first question can balance a negative answer to the second."

D. Elton Trueblood

Several years ago Carl Menk, Chairman of Canny, Bowes, Inc.—a prestigious executive search firm in New York City—sent me (Charles) a letter. He wrote to tell me about a survey that his firm had conducted recently among senior-level executives across America. The purpose of this study was to identify those personal qualities that top-level executives considered most vital to effective leadership. Carl's study was a carefully planned piece of research. Only those executives who had demonstrated a long pattern of accomplishments at high levels were invited to participate. Carl's firm had tracked the career progress of over one thousand senior-level executives for many years, so they knew who they were dealing with. In this survey each participant was asked to specify the characteristics they considered to be "very important," "important" or "less important" to success. After tabulating the data collected, Carl's firm found the following: Integrity topped the list as the most important quality. It was followed by ability to think conceptually and people skills. Decisiveness, intelligence, persuasiveness, and competitiveness were at or near the bottom of the list of traits.

The findings that Carl's study produced confirmed what an earlier survey revealed. One of these earlier studies was conducted by Korn Ferry, an internationally recognized executive search and consulting firm. Teaming up with researchers from UCLA's John E. Anderson School of Management, Korn Ferry people asked a select group of senior executives, "What quality do you think most necessary for business success?" Would you care to guess which trait these executives said was most responsible for enhancing a person's chances for success? That's right. It was integrity. Seventy-one percent of the senior executives surveyed said integrity was the most important quality.

Ask your friends what qualities come to mind when they hear the word integrity? We did; and this is what people told us: "A person with integrity lives by ideals." "What these people say and do is consistent." "They are not seduced by temptation." "They are more concerned with doing the right things than they are with getting things for themselves." These descriptions of integrity paint a picture of individuals who are undivided, whose actions are consistent with standards. It may interest you to know that the words *integrity* and *integer* have the same Latin origin, *integritas*, which means whole, complete. Perhaps the idea of integrity was best expressed by Socrates in the *Apology*. "A man who is good for anything," said Socrates, "ought not to calculate the chance of living or dying; he ought only to consider whether in doing anything he is doing right or wrong, acting the part of a good man or of a bad."

Few rewards in life are greater than being found worthy of the full trust of others. You may know of persons like this—friends in whom you have complete confidence. You know these persons will always take the honorable path. They would never give serious consideration to anything less. Temptations cannot budge them from their steadfast commitment to what's right and you trust them because of it. They enjoy your complete confidence because of their consistent dependability and truthfulness. They don't disappoint you; they don't let you down.

Integrity Rests upon *the Person Inside*

How we approach a difficult situation is not an insignificant matter. For one thing it reveals how we view ourselves and how we regard matters of right and wrong. For another thing our choices shape us and our ability to work with others. In studying the ways individuals handle matters of right and wrong, we've noticed two very different approaches. Let's consider the implications and consequences of each one.

On one side of the fence are the noncompromisers. These are the people who are willing to stand and fight for what they truly believe. Their beliefs are strong and rigidly held. These sturdy individuals will not bend under pressure and are impervious to intimidation. They cannot be bought, pestered, or persuaded into going against their own values. They insist on being who they see themselves as being and there is no changing that. Noncompromisers derive considerable satisfaction from knowing that they are authentic and highly principled. But, in this knowledge, they can easily grow smug and self-righteous. Moreover, in many ways, large and small, they can irritate others. They may even become unmanageable and uncooperative nuisances. Some of them turn into tyrannical bosses. One reason these people are so adamant in their stance is that they believe that who and what they are as persons is the accumulation of their everyday actions and habits. And they are not about to allow the slightest slipup to damage their spotless reputations or lead them to be disingenuous. Being persons of character is of the utmost importance to them. Sometimes they may be even more concerned with their own authenticity and integrity than they are with the larger purposes of their organizations.

On the other side of the fence are the compromisers. They might stretch the truth to get their way, choose work that they hate because it pays handsomely, or act in phony ways just to please others and get what they want. Faustian bargains don't trouble them. They willingly do whatever it takes to accomplish their purposes. While these people may find compromise-demanding situations troubling, ultimately they give in. They turn a blind eye to those principles and standards that underlie authenticity and integrity. These people are compromisers because they measure their worth as humans in terms of the positions they occupy, the accomplishments they have achieved, and the material rewards they have earned. And, when it is all said and done, many of these people get what they set out to attain. They move ahead in organizations precisely because they are effective at doing what their organizations want them to do. They can earn handsome pay packages when they produce outstanding results, despite their methods. While they may earn the outward measures of success, every compromise they make holds the possibility of diminishing their self-respect, the admiration others might otherwise have for them, and their sense of lasting fulfillment.

It is hard to think of anything that individuals can do that is more important to the quality of life for their families, friends, and country than that of acting with integrity. Nothing enables a person to achieve a well-adjusted personality and avoid self-inflicted troubles better than simple honesty. Why then is integrity so rare among us? One reason is that mere knowledge of what's right and wrong is not enough. There is considerable agreement as to what's good or bad in the abstract sense: stealing is wrong, lying is wrong, meanness is wrong, greed is bad, and so on. Also, we know that just because it is within a person's power to choose freely what is right, it does not follow that it is always easy to do so. Of course, it is easy to seek revenge, to take another's possessions, to say things that are known to be false, to pay or accept bribes. Likewise, it is also easy to do a good and right thing from time to time: to show compassion, tell the truth, refuse to go along with an underhanded scheme. What's difficult for humans is to choose right actions over wrong ones consistently. Long ago, in ancient Greece, Aristotle (384–322 BC) came to this conclusion in Book V of *The Nichomachean Ethics*, where he wrote, "It is easy to perform a good action, but not so easy to acquire a settled habit of performing such actions." Good habits do not come to us naturally or easily. We acquire them in only one way, by acting. The secret behind the formation of good habits is steadfast consistency in one's actions—no exceptions, no excuses.

Sooner or later you will face an ethical dilemma and be forced to decide what to do. If you are wise, you will proceed with your eyes wide open, your mind fully engaged to understand the costs and consequences associated with each possible choice. Your courage and creativity will be tested to come up with smart responses. But ultimately you will realize that the greatest difficulty is that you must give up something to get something else that you deem more important. We've seen many fine individuals who are scrupulously honest about little things but who cave in when it comes to big things. Consider the salesperson who would never think of fudging on reported travel expenses or misrepresenting the quality features of a product. Yet what happens when this same salesperson is under pressure from higher-ups to sell additional product lines? Will that same salesperson make promises knowing full well they cannot be kept? Will that salesperson say things that aren't true about their product or a rival's product? Does the salesperson quit? Or, does the salesperson go ahead with what's asked just to hold on to a well-paid job? Everyone who lives and works in our imperfect world knows that wisdom and judgment are vital to effective performance and being able to sleep at night with a clean conscience. Regardless of the situation, one must be willing to face the fact that doing what's right will always extract a price.

How can we explain a person's integrity? Where does it come from? How might one develop a settled habit of right-minded action? From our own lives we realize that our actions always run through our minds and hearts before they are played out. The key to living with integrity rests on both wanting the right things and making the right choices. The way to integrity starts by thoughtful inspection of one's self—one's motives, drives, desires, goals. The way to integrity also involves overcoming four destructive obstacles: (1) desires born of selfishness, (2) the relativist's attitude that right and wrong are a matter of personal opinion, (3) taking "the easy way out" by ignoring moral problems, and (4) pursuing the approval of others to gain popularity. These are the chief ways in which people harm their reputations and cause others to mistrust them.

The Devil of Immediate Desires

On May 25, 2006, in a Houston courtroom, a jury found two men guilty of fraud, making false statements, conspiracy, and insider trading. It was one of the biggest corporate scandals in U.S. history. The verdict sent a message across America: No matter how smart and powerful you are, you cannot lie to shareholders. These men were not common thugs or hardened street criminals. They were highly educated individuals; who, when their company was turning in record profits, were held in high regard by Wall Street and prominent members of their communities. They were sophisticated, smooth, well-connected, and smart—maybe too smart. One held a doctorate in economics from a major university and the other an MBA from one of the nation's most prestigious business schools.

Earlier, in a detailed account of the events leading up to this indictment, *Fortune* writers Bethany McLean and Peter Elkind wrote a book about these men and the others who created and ran Enron. It chronicled the events that led to the rise and eventual collapse of the energy giant in 2001, calling the men at the top, "the smartest guys in the room." Yet, on that Thursday morning in 2006, when their trial ended, it was painfully clear that there is something of far greater importance than smartness. Their heads slumped down as they heard the jury's verdict, because Jeffrey Skilling and the late Kenneth Lay understood at that moment that they might be spending the remainder of their lives behind bars.

As you read this chapter, right now, there are thousands of people around the globe thinking to themselves, "I wish I hadn't done it. I really didn't think I'd get caught." Whatever it was that any one of these people did, each now is thinking, "Why was I so dumb as to do it? It was wrong and I knew it. Yet I did it anyway." The people who confront this fate might even include ourselves. One reason why people do things they know are wrong is that they hand control of their lives over to the devil of immediate desires. This devil's trickery is fairly simple to understand. Here is how he operates. First, he convinces us that we can get whatever we want doing anything we want and get away with it undetected, untarnished. Next, the devil of immediate desires fans the flames, so to speak, of our greedy impulses. Before we realize it, our impulses have grown so intense that they have gotten beyond our capacity to control them. And if these moves are not quite enough to get us to go over the edge and cause us to yield to our wants, the devil of immediate desires whispers into our hearts, "Go ahead. You deserve these things you crave. You can get them by any means you choose and not get caught."

One of the chief reasons why the devil of immediate desires is so successful in defeating people is that he delivers on his promises. People do get away with using dishonest or downright mean methods to secure what they want. You might know of someone who operates in these kinds of ways. Here is something else you might see in them. After a while it grows easier for these people to give in to their desires. Their pattern of doing whatever they want to get what they want becomes easier for them to stomach. Then things turn worse. These people become so inoculated from using their moral compasses that they become disoriented from what's right and good. Each time they get away with employing dishonorable methods it grows easier for them to use them again, and then again. After a while it becomes less uncomfortable for an individual to follow underhanded ways. But something even more distressing happens to persons who follow this kind of pattern: They gradually come to believe that they are above the rules and standards that everyone else is expected to follow. These people convince themselves that they are special, above the standards of right and wrong.

If the past provides a reliable indication of what will occur in the future, we can expect more men and women will come to ruin by failing to control their ambition. The Greeks had a word for the source of these people's downfall, hubris. It means excessive pride, arrogance. It can grow out of control in the hearts of practically everyone. Hubris is rooted in the belief that one is so smart and so powerful that civilization's ideals and standards simply do not apply to them. Like Roman emperors, who actually believed they were gods, those with hubris believe that they can do whatever they want, and do it to whomever they want, without repercussions. History teaches us that if all one values is one's own smartness and power and things material, then, just like a Roman god, there is no need to control one's self. That's what hubris leads one to believe.

In recent years you have probably read numerous accounts of greedy, self-serving individuals running some of America's best-known companies. Dennis Kozlowski, former CEO of Tyco, comes to mind as a supreme example. During "his ten-year reign of greed," as *Fortune* magazine put it, Kozlowski "spared no expense as he used corporate money to adorn his corporate offices and his numerous personal residences." His extravagances included a $20 million birthday party for his wife (he reportedly charged $10 million of this to his company because many of the guests there were Tyco employees), a $6,000 shower curtain and $15,000 for each umbrella stand in his home. Discovered by auditors, authorities charged Kozlowski with pilfering $400 million from company coffers. In the end Kozlowski and his CFO Mark Swartz, left Tyco's reputation in tatters, its financial condition in terrible shape.

Most cheating and wrongdoing involves petty, everyday little things, not the massive fraud that we read about in newspapers. Yet the hubris behind big-time swindlers and penny-ante cheats is exactly the same, and it is just as self-defeating. Whether they do it in big ways or small, those who cheat others usually exhibit a certain level of arrogance, a feeling that they are above the laws and standards of morality. A simple illustration of hubris came to our attention recently. It involved a man, we'll call him Joe, who once showed up for a job interview with our friend Gail. When Joe entered Gail's office to be interviewed, she thought from the way he was dressed that he was a used car salesman. A minute into the interview she learned that her immediate impression was accurate. Indeed, he once was a used car salesman. After asking the usual questions to learn about Joe's employment history, Gail asked him if he had any other sales experience. "Oh yes," he said. "Have you ever been to the Caribbean and bought one of those 14 karat gold charms?"

"Why, yes, as a matter of fact I have," she replied. "Do you sell those?"

"Yes. Would you like to buy some?"

"Are they really 14 karat gold?" Gail asked him.

"No. They aren't 14 karat. That's what we tell people, but they will never find out," he said.

Gail was taken aback. She paused a moment to collect her thoughts. "You know what?" she said. "I think this interview is over."

Defeating the Devil of Immediate Desires

Long ago Jim Casey, the man who founded United Parcel Service and served as its chairman and CEO for many years, made a profound observation. "I sometimes think it unfortunate," said Casey, "that so many kinds of business transactions must be measured in terms of money. For, in each transaction involving money, our selfish motives are apt to take possession of us and tempt us to act in ways detrimental to someone else. We may easily fail to recognize that our obligations run two ways, in that we should give and get full value for every penny exchanged."

We think Mr. Casey put his finger on the root cause of many troubles. It is selfishness. How many people do you know who are consumed with the concern, *What's in it for me?* We examined numerous instances where successful business leaders ably demonstrated high levels of integrity. What do you suppose they all did to overcome their selfish impulses? They took a good, hard look at the situation they were in, not from their own position but from the other person's perspective. In an article appearing in *Business Week* recently, someone asked Jack Welch, former CEO of General Electric, what he thought made a great salesperson. His answer was, first and foremost, *empathy for the customer*. A great salesman looks at a sale from the perspective of the customer and, when all the bargaining is over each party can say the deal was fair. We cannot think of a better way of overcoming self-defeating tendencies born of selfishness than by developing a sincere concern for the other person. How many times have you seen people get themselves into trouble because they worried first about themselves and then, if it occurred to them at all, considered the interests of the person with whom they were dealing? Just imagine all the difficulties that could be avoided if this thought pattern were turned the other way around.

Walter Haas, Jr., who ran Levi Strauss & Company in San Francisco for many years, just as his father had done before him, once told me (Charles) about an experience he had shortly after World War II. It happened when a man named Stafford and his son, from Sedalia, Missouri, called on Walter's father, who was running Levi's at the time. The Staffords had a business, the J. A. Lamy Manufacturing Company, and were looking for contract production. Could their firm sew Levis on contract? Stafford and the senior Haas talked for a while and struck an agreement: J. A. Lamy Manufacturing would produce a hundred dozen trousers a day. Stafford and Haas shook hands and the bargain was sealed.

On their drive home later that day, Walter, Jr., said to his father, "Dad, I saw the figures you agreed to with the Staffords and I know we could have gotten that production for ten cents a dozen less than you agreed to pay." The senior Haas told his son, "I could probably have done better than that. What you have to understand, son, is that when you make a contract with someone, both sides have got to be happy with it. And, the Staffords are happy with it. And because they're happy with it, I expect that one of these days we'll get another five hundred dozen in that plant." A few years later, they did.

Another illustration of this powerful idea—of being just as concerned with what's in a bargain for the other person as you are with what's in it for yourself—comes from an experience of the Brunswick Corporation, located north of Chicago. Brunswick once came out with a new, high-performance bowling ball. These balls became an instant success. Amateur bowlers loved them. The professionals who picked them up began winning tournaments, one after another. Endorsements from top money-winning bowlers sell bowling balls, lots of them. But success was short-lived. It was found that these balls were susceptible to heat. Left in the trunk of a car on a hot day, the cover would soften. It is impossible to bowl with a marshmallow! Upon learning of the problem, Brunswick CEO Jack Reichert, responded immediately: "Recall every ball."

Corporate accountants scurried in to Reichert's office with their calculations. It could cost Brunswick over a million dollars. Reichert persisted, "Good, recall them all with a full cash refund to customers." By the time all refunds were made, the cost to Brunswick totaled $2.5 million. Throughout the ordeal Reichert's words sounded loud and clear, "If our name means anything to a customer, when you make a mistake you've got to pay for it."

The powers that people like Jack Reichert, Walter Haas, Sr., and Jim Casey—and thousands of others who have done similar good things—used to overcome self-centeredness came in the form of a much-talked about, ancient idea: the Golden Rule. The essence of the Golden Rule is that each one of us ought to be as much concerned with our neighbor's well-being as we are with our own. The ideal is to be impartial. This is not altruism, which places the welfare of others ahead of self. What we are talking about here is evenhanded treatment. This means that I should be impartial and not make a distinction between my own well-being and the well-being of my neighbor.

The Seductiveness of Relativism

In every office, shop, and factory across our nation there are to be found inviting possibilities to pursue what thoughtful men and women will disagree about as to whether they are right or wrong. The financial officer of a small company going through tough times at the moment—we'll call her Jean—ordered company accountants not to "write off" unusable inventory (record its fair market value) because doing so would reduce reported earnings and consequently have a negative effect on the firm's stock price. Jean tells herself that this is just a temporary bending of accounting rules and that she will adjust the inventory figure to reflect the correct amount next year when sales and earnings are expected to be much better. Jean knows that whenever market observers find small declines in a company's earnings the "bad news" leads to irrational overreaction—stock prices fall way beyond reason. She feels that having the company stock take a sharp dive downward is not in anyone's best interest when it isn't, in her opinion, warranted. It's better to avoid hurting investors, Jean believes, so she instructs her people to act accordingly.

Your mind might contain the seeds of ideas that could develop into self-defeating tendencies. A popular notion that affects many lives in destructive ways today is the ideal of trying to be seen as "open-minded." Open-mindedness, as many view it, means being accepting of all standards and beliefs. Many people think that if we were all more open-minded and accepting of differing beliefs, our increased tolerance would eliminate conflict and discord. Just the other day I watched a television program that contained a segment on a man who had several wives. Each wife had children by him. This "family" appeared quite happy with their arrangement. Now the man wants to add an additional "wife" to the household. I suppose that those who espouse "open-mindedness" would say that we should be accepting of what these people are doing. After all, we aren't being harmed ourselves. Or are we? By accepting any and all standards of conduct, could we in fact be harming ourselves?

A very wise person once pointed out to me (Charles) that there is a big difference between accepting another human being lovingly and accepting a person's unlovely actions. It is one thing to accept a person, to value that person's humanity. It is quite another thing to accept a person's behavior. Mothers and fathers know what it means to love their children and to scold them at the same time. You might want to think more about what being "open to all points of view and beliefs" entails. Our experience suggests that this primitive notion of tolerance, which we are examining here, leads to disturbing conclusions: (1) There really is no certainty as to which standard of conduct is correct and best. So, we are free to choose whichever standards suit our fancy at the moment. (2) Since it is supremely important to accept others and be accepted by them, we ought not to offend others by suggesting that we believe our ways and beliefs are superior to theirs. We need to accept the idea that any standard or point of view is just as good as any other one. It's all relative. These beliefs are at the heart of what's known as "relativism." What relativists fail to grasp is that just because a person firmly believes that a particular standard or ideal or point of view is best or true or most correct, it does not follow that he or she is intolerant of others who see things differently. It does not mean that the person with deeply held convictions cannot coexist harmoniously with those who believe differently.

The Fallacies of Relativism

We can just imagine how Jean, the financial officer, mentioned in the previous section, would find comfort in the relativist's way of thinking. It would afford her an easy out, a way to escape blame. Can you see any harm in this? We think there is harm. For relativism keeps humans from a full and honest assessment of themselves and their actions. Relativism seduces people into doing whatever they feel like doing. They will grasp for whatever they most want at the moment and try to hold on to it by any means. Afterward, they defend their actions by creating nice-sounding reasons to justify their purposes and methods. The person who accepts everything as equally good or correct may consider herself tolerant and open-minded, but in fact she never thinks at all. What the relativist considers tolerance is in reality a form of closed mindedness—he never opens his mind to struggle with difficult questions having to do with how one ought to behave.

You can observe for yourself, in everyday encounters, examples aplenty that will convince you of the reality of right and wrong. The next time you witness a heated argument pay attention to what each adversary says to the other. Just the other day, while waiting in a long line, we observed a man cutting in ahead of a woman: "Hey, who do you think you are, crowding ahead of everyone else in line? Wait your turn, just like everyone else." One man told us of a time when a family tried to crowd ahead of people at an airport who were waiting to check in for a flight. This man told us that the family's action made him so angry that he stood up and in a loud voice said. "Ladies and gentlemen, I'd like to introduce the Pig Family to you. This is Mr. Pig. This is Mrs. Pig, and these are the Pig's children." In another instance a neighbor told us of an unpleasant experience he had with a repair service: "You promised me that if this dishwasher broke within six months, you'd come out and fix it at no charge. I'm not paying this bill. It isn't right for you to charge me."

As you listen to these kinds of squabbles, you will hear something else, something you might consider astounding. You will always find that there is much more to the argument than one person's behavior displeasing another person. Each party will argue that their opponent has violated some rule by which they think the world ought to operate. You can always bet it is a rule which favors their position. Sometimes too, people will argue that "there is no rule," so they can do just as they please. Each party says that the other person is in the "wrong." Each will claim that their adversary did something that should not be done. What can these disputes teach us? We can be sure that everyone, even the most hardened criminal, believes that universal standards of right and wrong exist, regardless of whether we know what they are. Even the worst elements of society would prefer an ordered world structured on right and wrong to a disordered world that is not.

You might think that highly educated people would be the first to agree to the simple idea that right and wrong exist. Not true. Many believe that the world is simply too complex for such simple ideas as good and bad, right and wrong to exist at all. In an essay, Christina Hoff Sommers wrote about a personal experience. At the time of this incident Professor Sommers was teaching philosophy at Clark University. Sommers had been having a running debate with one of her colleagues. Her colleague's position was that morality is relative—that right and wrong are a matter of personal opinion. Professor Sommers saw things differently. She believed that some things are right and others are wrong. One day Professor Sommers encountered her colleague, who was quite angry and upset. "What's the problem?" Sommers inquired. "It's the students," her colleague replied. "I just looked at their term papers. They plagiarized." The students had broken a rule—a rule that she honored.

A person does not need a whole lot of schooling to know that some things are clearly wrong. Lying is wrong. Stealing is wrong. Cheating is wrong. Being a nuisance is wrong. Other things are right. Telling the truth is right. Being kind is right. Giving your best effort is right. Playing fair and by the rules is right. What makes something right or wrong does not depend on the circumstances or your personal opinion. Socrates said it this way: "There is a real and objective right, wholly independent of our opinions and wishes, which it is our whole duty to try to discover."

If you want a practical guide for determining whether an action is ethical, here is a suggestion. Many people call it the *New York Times* test, which they use before deciding and acting. It goes like this: Pretend that tomorrow morning's newspaper will have your decision or action described in full detail. If you are okay with having millions of people read about what you did, then it is probably ethical. A word of caution is in order here. Don't allow the fear of getting caught for doing wrong to be the main reason for acting ethically. A person of integrity will refuse to act despicably simply because it is wrong to do so. Still, it is helpful to imagine how others might judge your actions. This is because in doing so you will bring high-minded thoughts into your head that can crowd out your selfish desires. Another useful guide for making ethical choices is Immanuel Kant's Categorical Imperative. Drawing upon biblical principles, Kant (1724–1804) gave us a simple test to use in making ethical choices. It is this: If you do not think it right for everyone else to do what you are thinking of doing, then that action is unethical. You should act in such a way that it would be okay for everyone else in the world to act likewise. According to Kant no one is above the laws of right and wrong. Therefore, one should never make himself an exception to these standards for his own convenience or wants. If people like Ken Lay, Jeff Skilling, and Dennis Kozlowski had followed Kant's Categorical Imperative, the damage done to their companies—particularly to the employees and investors—would never have occurred.

The Perils of Turning a "Blind Eye" to Potential Ethical Problems

With work pressures what they are and with so many demands pressing in on us, it is easy to ignore hints of possible ethical problems yet to come. Yet, as we all know, it's better to stop something going bad when it is small, before it grows large and out of control. We hear about something going on that's wrong or receive small hints of it, and how do we respond? This is not a time to allow passivity to rule the day. Our advice is, "Act. And act quickly." Here is a simple illustration of what we mean.

Rodger, a salesperson at a local automobile agency we know of, once overheard technicians talking about a serious defect in one of the used cars, an SUV on the lot, as he walked through the service area. Actually, what Rodger heard was one technician telling another that an SUV on the used lot had a problem with the motor that shifts the vehicle from two-wheel to four-wheel drive. The technician remarked that the problem was erratic; it happened only once that he knew about. Still, it would be very expensive to repair. Several days after overhearing this bit of information, a customer came on the lot, looked at SUVs and found one he really liked. The customer made him a reasonable offer on it. Rodger assured the prospective buyer that the vehicle was in fine operating order. He really did not know with 100 percent certainty whether the SUV his customer offered to purchase was the one with the problem. Nor did he know it was not the one with the problem. So, by remaining ignorant and uncertain about the true nature of this particular vehicle, he went ahead with the deal, feeling it was okay because he just did not know the full story.

It is inescapable: there is always a cost associated with every choice you make, particularly when the choice has moral implications. Extra effort might cost Rodger a much-wanted commission. But that's only one of the costs he should consider. There are other costs that deserve attention too—his reputation, his self-respect, his customer's well-being, damage to his employer's reputation, damage to the image of business in general. You can stop the possibility of getting into serious ethical difficulties down the road by acting immediately when hints of trouble first appear and the problem is still small and solvable.

The head of an aerospace company told us about a time when his firm was charged with paying bribes to officials of a foreign government to secure contracts to build aircraft. Although he was not involved with it and had no evidence that such behavior was going on, this executive said that he had heard "rumblings" through the company grapevine that persons inside his organization might be offering under-the-table payments. When the bribes were exposed and his company was forced to pay fines for breaking U.S. laws, this executive lamented that he should have been more diligent. He said that he was very busy at the time and did not look into it. In retrospect, he wished that he had been more aggressive and stopped it before it happened. You can build trust between yourself and others and develop a reputation for honesty if you follow this prescription: Be vigilant. Act "right" before unnoticed bad things are allowed to proceed and become big, embarrassing problems.

Get Ahead of Problems—Nip Them in the Bud

When one makes a mistake, even an honest slipup because of ignorance, the question is, "Should I bring it out into the open and try to correct it even though doing so might be costly?" Here's an illustration of acting wisely before the potential future problem could grow large. A salesperson we heard about once sold an office chair to a customer who really would have preferred a taller model than the one that was actually ordered and delivered. Perhaps the salesperson made a mistake by not looking into the available options more fully and finding that a taller model was available. Nonetheless, the customer ordered the shorter version of the chair and it was delivered. Later on, the salesperson learned that a taller model of the chair had always been available. But by now the customer had already gotten the shorter version of the chair and was using it. What to do? The salesperson realized that to remain "mum" would risk being discovered and a damaged reputation could result. So the salesperson called the customer, "fessed up" to the error and offered the customer the option of returning the new chair, now in use, and receiving in its place the preferred model.

The secret of developing a good reputation may be as simple as addressing potential problems immediately in an open and forthright manner. When he headed Zenith Corporation, John Nevin once chose to deal with a possible public relations nightmare head-on, in an open and direct way. The situation involved a television failure and it all began one day when the senior engineering executive walked into Nevin's office. He closed the door and said, "John, we have a failure and it's more serious than any of us imagined. There's reason to believe we might have a radiation problem." In a series of recent tests, Zenith engineers detected small amounts of radiation being emitted from its color television sets. Zenith had a long tradition of being a reliable company and its senior executives knew that few things would strike greater terror in a mother and father than having their child sit in front of a radiation hazard.

Twenty-four hours later, John Nevin was on a plane from Chicago, headed to Washington, D. C. There he would meet with people from the U.S. Department of Radiological Health and explain everything they knew. The regulatory bodies in Washington, D.C. have a procedure that, by law, they must follow to establish that a manufacturer is not in conformity with the radiation standards. If the regulatory agency concludes that the radiation standards are not being met, the manufacturer has an opportunity to protest. If the protest fails, then there is a formal investigation of whether there is a health hazard. But these steps take time, as both Zenith executives and regulators knew. Zenith and the regulators therefore agreed immediately to waive all these procedures and move directly to testing sets for radiation hazards. They set up the procedures with government scientists and Zenith engineers.

When the initial tests had been completed the regulatory agency issued its finding, saying "Zenith has found certain of its receivers ... to be not in conformity with radiation standards. The Bureau is now beginning an investigation to determine if there were any possible adverse health effects." Within three months enough testing had been completed to enable the Bureau to issue a bulletin saying that the worst impact on the consumer would be the equivalent of the radiation dosage equal to what one gets with a dental X-ray.

The Pursuit of Popularity

A great many problems that people cause for themselves come by way of exactly the same capacity that enables them to be aware of themselves. We all know that we are able to inspect our own behavior, which frequently leads to our own betterment. In addition, this same ability allows us to visualize how others will regard us. We realize that, as humans, we are primarily social creatures, needing to belong, to be accepted by others. We all want to be liked and appreciated. We love whatever praise comes our way. These desires are not all bad. In fact, they can be quite good for us. Social forces discourage our antisocial urges and promote civility.

To a large degree how people regard themselves is determined by how they think others regard them. Very seldom do our finest actions arise from absolutely unmixed motives. Notice how attuned you are to what's going on around you. Notice how you consider how your words will be received by others before you speak. You choose your tone and what you say. Notice that you also think about what you want others to think of you. You will not simply try to protect your reputation but will also consciously try to "project" the image that you want others to have of you. In truth, like everyone else, you will do things, expecting certain benefits in return. Yes, we are very calculating creatures—and much of what we calculate is how to receive the praise, the acceptance, and the recognition we crave from others. We give generously and then expect a reward. We do nice things anticipating favorable responses from those we help. The truth is that oftentimes what we most want is not the actual fruits of our efforts but to bask contentedly in the sunshine of our own self-approval and the praise of others.

Who can say that this is all bad? It probably isn't. But be careful. It is from this same motive—expecting something in return—that many people bend to popular opinion, doing what they think will gain applause. Winning the approval of others is not always a clear gain. Many people have damaged their reputations irreparably by pursuing popularity for themselves instead of what better judgment would regard as wise. Often, what's popular with others is just plain wrong. Those who act in ways designed primarily to win praise from the masses frequently meet disastrous consequences. How often we hear of unpopular decisions that were once condemned by popular opinion but were judged by history to be prudent. What clamoring crowds once demanded be done has frequently, later on, proved to be just plain wrong.

You might find yourself doing things that don't feel right on the inside to secure the approval of others or get something you want on the outside. The desire for acceptance and approval can become a terrible force in any situations, but is especially harmful in work settings. We've seen people turn on their coworkers—gossiping about them, looking for their faults, hoping to find ways of causing them to be fired or disciplined, spreading false rumors about what they said or did. Victims of such maneuvers become outcasts. An outcast is easy prey for others to gang up on and do mean things to in order to gain group popularity for themselves.

Another way a person can harm herself is to lie to potential customers in order to make a sale and win favor with higher-ups. One woman we know of worked for a business that trains young girls in how to be models. The saleswoman we heard about would tell mothers, "Your little girl is darling. She's a natural for a career in modeling. We can show her what she needs to be able to get big money contracts. Sign her up for our course."

Learn to "Just Say No!"

One of our students, a woman named Mary, told of her experience working behind the counter for a major car rental company at the Columbus, Ohio, Airport. Her primary responsibility was to convince unsuspecting customers to purchase extra insurance for the cars they were renting. The manager instructed Mary *not* to make the point that the $12 insurance charge was per diem, just that the charge for insurance was $12. Mary was told to say, "Would you like this insurance for $12?" and, *not to say* "for $12 per day." It was the rental company's method of making more money. Mary told us that in her view the rental company took advantage of the elderly, those who were in a hurry, and those who did not understand the rental contract. Now when customers returned their vehicles and found what they owed on their bills, they were outraged. Between having to face her conscience, which was tormented by having to use deceptive tactics being imposed by managers above her, and the unhappy customers, angry about their bills, Mary decided to leave her job. "I just could not do it," she said.

In the years immediately following World War II the managing director of Caterpillar's European operations in Grenoble, France, searched desperately for a suitable apartment. The housing situation at the time was extremely tight. The city was bursting with people and decent accommodations were scarce. After considerable searching, he finally located an apartment to buy. It was a brand new, seven-room suite on the sixth floor of the Park Hotel. When the manager and the owner's agents got to negotiating the final price, which had tentatively been agreed to already, the negotiator for the seller brought up something else. He said, "Well, of course there's the "accommodating payment" to give you priority to get this apartment." This was the first time anything like that had been brought up. At that, Caterpillar's managing director stood up, said, "This meeting is adjourned. I don't want your apartment," and he walked out. Word of this incident permeated the whole community. It let everyone know from that time on that if you were dealing with Caterpillar in general, or its managing director in particular, everything would have to be on the up-and-up, open and aboveboard.

Face Yourself Honestly

Not long ago in our area a young man named Todd was found doing something unethical where he worked and upper management fired him for it. Todd worked at the entrance gate of a beach water park where he sold entry passes. A local FM radio station ran a promotion that summer, sending coupons to their listeners, who could then go to the water park, present their coupon and receive a discount on their admission. The station broadcast at 98 megahertz—thus the 98-cent discount. Todd discovered that the water park's control procedures were lax and he took advantage of this. Most of the people who came to the water park did not have a discount coupon, so they paid the regular admission price, which is $24. When Todd took their money, he rang up $23.02 at his cash register and pocketed the 98 cents. Over the many weeks he worked at the water park, he took in a few thousand dollars for himself. What's more, he told others who worked at the entrance gate that they too could do the same thing and get away with it. His scheme worked for most of the summer but someone got wind of it, investigated the matter and Todd was found out and fired on the spot.

In talking to Todd afterward, he said this:

> I'm not a bad person. Actually, I'm a lot better than most people I know. But let's face it. Everyone needs to look out for himself. Sometimes that isn't very nice. I don't see the world in terms of black and white. There are exceptions to every rule. Nobody's perfect anyway. Besides, what harm is it to the water park? They make lots of money anyway—what I did is no big deal.

How often we hear people inventing excuses for their actions, attempting to give a reason for their errant ways. Are you an excuse maker? As you examine yourself and your actions, guard against making up nice-sounding excuses—excuses which weaken any chance you have to examine yourself with uncompromising honesty. These excuses are the handiwork of the *devil of self-deception*. Here are the kinds of thoughts this devil puts into our heads for us to use to excuse our actions:

- I was a *victim of necessity*. I had no other options.
- I made *an innocent error*. It was just a bureaucratic snafu. I didn't intend to do it.
- He tells himself, "I'll make an *exception* here. Just this once I'll ignore the rules, I'll bend the truth, or I'll violate standards and agreements. It won't hurt to do it this *one* time only."
- It's okay because it is the *established pattern* in this industry (or that country, so it really isn't illegal or immoral.
- I had to do it for *self-preservation*. The thought is, "We can do anything if it is necessary to preserve our existence."
- I had to do it in order to *protect my self-interest*. "It was in the best interests of the company therefore we were expected to do it. In fact, we

probably ought to be rewarded for doing what's best for the business." The argument is: "one must do whatever it takes to survive."

- I *won't be found out*. No one will ever know. "I'll keep it a secret." By escaping detection, I'm home free.
- What I did *was really unselfish*. Although it broke the law to sell it to them, my customer needed the product.
- *It is too difficult* to follow every little rule. I can't spend all my time worrying about whether I violate insignificant laws or ethical standards.
- I acted that way because *that's just the way I am*. I'm just being myself.
- I know I was wrong, but *I cannot control myself*. The impulse was just too strong for me to resist.
- I am a complex person with extraordinary talents and these sometimes go against conventional standards that others follow. But if I am to accomplish great things, *I must be free to express myself freely, the way I do*.
- What I do really doesn't make all that much difference in the great scheme of things. *I'm just one individual*.

BE OF SERVICE TO OTHERS

Rise Above Indifference, Have an Ultimate Concern That Goes Beyond Your Self, Serve Others Generously

"Man's highest distinction is the service of others."

George VI of Great Britain

In his accounts of the Persian Wars, Herodotus tells of the time when Croesus, king of the Lydian empire at the height of its prosperity in the sixth century BC, invited Solon, the Athenian lawgiver, to come to Sardis and be received there as his guest in the royal palace. Solon accepted. Passing through the court, Solon thought each nobleman, richly dressed and attended to by a multitude of guards and footboys, was the king. Finally Solon was brought before Croesus, who was adorned with every imaginable rarity and curiosity—jewels, gold, and purple—and making a grand and glorious spectacle of himself. Solon didn't express the slightest amazement at all the wealth he saw. Nor did he lavish compliments on Croesus, as the king was accustomed to receiving. Whereupon, Croesus commanded that all his treasure houses be opened for Solon to inspect. Surely after seeing with his own eyes the king's sumptuous furniture and luxuries Solon would acknowledge their greatness and magnificence. But Solon was not dazzled by the display of opulence which had awed so many others.

On the third or fourth day, after Solon had gazed upon the vast and glorious treasures, Croesus asked the wise and well-traveled Athenian a leading question: "Stranger of Athens, whom, of all men that you have seen, do you consider the most happy?" This the king asked because he thought, surely, he was the happiest of all mortals. Solon answered the king truthfully and without flattery—"Tellus of Athens, sire," answered Solon. This answer must have baffled Croesus. He pressed Solon again. "Who, after Tellus, seemed to him to be the happiest?" The Lydian king thought he'd at least be given second place. But when Solon answered, "Cleobis and Bito," the king thought him to be a fool.

We are told that Solon's answers angered Croesus. Didn't his treasuries of gold and silver count for more than these other men's honor and public admiration? He could not comprehend why Solon was so dismissive of his ideal of happiness. Solon acknowledged the obvious, saying to Croesus, "I see that you are wonderfully rich and lord of many nations." But he cautioned against saluting as happy one who is still in the midst of life and hazards and believes possessions can be a fortress for securing safety and comfort.

You can ruin your life or you can make it rich. It all depends on what you choose to pursue. There are objects aplenty that glisten and attract and substances that anesthetize the senses. It is tragically easy to be blinded by harmful and limiting forces that mislead humans from the depths and grandeur of what life's experiences can offer them. In our busy, noisy, self-focused, competitive world many people devote their efforts exclusively to just one thing, getting. Day after day their concerns focus on just one question: what must I do to get what I want? Sadly, these people miss out on experiencing anything beyond themselves and what they want. For them, work is purely an economic exchange. Effort is doled out for an agreed-upon price. To them, nothing is beyond commercialization. They are calculating in all they do. They are preoccupied with just one thing, "getting." Because they operate this way they merely exist, unexcited and uninspired by anything beyond their own immediate needs.

The Aim of Making Yourself Happy

One of the most destructive inner drives humans can have is that of being overly concerned with their own happiness. Like Croesus, many people today focus their primary attention on one thing, making themselves happy. This drive can crowd out all other motives and become an obsession. The sad truth is that overwhelming concern for one's personal happiness is a telling symptom of something that is terribly wrong within a human being. While it might sound odd to label happiness a problem, a problem it is. Of course we would all rather be happy than sad. But the direct pursuit of happiness for its own sake is self-defeating.

The examples of countless persons reveal to us an important truth: happiness does not come from what one gets in the way of things material or from the praises of others. It comes from following something each of us can develop from within ourselves. Paradoxically, the greatest unhappiness also comes from within. It comes from focusing attention on ourselves, from worrying about our own happiness. Elton Trueblood once pointed out that most of those whom we honor in history have been strangely uninterested in the question of whether they were personally happy. Our heroes are men and women who have cared about justice or truth and have not even raised the happiness question at all. Of course, many of them have actually been gloriously happy, but it is not happiness at which they aimed. Their happiness came from giving their lives to some worthy cause and serving that cause unhesitatingly. To get happiness you must forget about it.

We once asked over one hundred of our country's most successful CEOs of the largest and best respected companies a question: "What has given you the greatest satisfaction in your career?" Do you know what they told us? It wasn't their pay and bonuses, which ran into the millions. It wasn't the power and prestige that came with their responsibilities. Nor was it the satisfaction of being able to sit atop some mighty enterprise. No, it was none of the things that the average person in the street might expect. Here is a sampling of what these leaders said.

- "It's having a reason for being on earth. You've got to live a constructive life."
- "It isn't living for yourself. It is adding to the lives of others."
- "It's taking care of others—those who depend on you."
- "The important idea here is not, "What can I get with what I've got?" Instead it is, "What can I do with what I've got?"
- "It is taking what God gave you in the way of talent and maximizing it over as much time as God gives you to live."

One specific suggestion that you will find useful in escaping the destructiveness of self-centeredness is to stop what you are doing and examine your own thoughts. Here are some destructive worries people generally have that you can watch out for: "Am I getting ahead fast enough? Are others getting a better deal than I'm getting? Do I get to have the final say in things? Am I getting my way? Are things convenient for me, giving me the least amount of trouble and irritation?" Do these questions sound familiar? Can you spot what's at the core of them? That's right. It's "me"—me, me, me. It would be a terrible mistake to think we ought not to be concerned about ourselves. We should be. But self-centeredness is something else entirely; it is destructive in any workplace. The self-centered person is unwilling to cooperate; unwilling to give her finest efforts toward the attainment of her work unit's goals if she is not in 100 percent agreement with them; and not willing to sacrifice her convenience in order to accommodate the wants and needs of others.

Dominating Desire Matters

Whenever you peer into a human heart you will find something at its core dominating it. One of the best ways of improving the quality of your performance at work is to make top-notch quality that best serves the customer your uppermost concern. Not long ago while searching for someone to build a set of doors for a large public building, a knowledgeable person recommended a local company. We went to see their shop foreman, the man who would be in charge of the project. With our plan in hand, we showed the foreman what we had in mind. He studied it for a while and said that he would not build the doors that our plans called for. "I won't let work like that come out of my shop," he told us. He went on to explain why: the materials called for would not stand up to the weather; the structural design was defective—the stiles in our design were not wide enough to carry the load; the diamond-shaped panels our plan called for would, in time, lead to unavoidable shrinkage and let in moisture, causing the wood to rot. It was just a bad design all around: he was not about to allow such a piece of work to be built in his shop. Another door design would be needed. Then he'd do the job—in a way that he respected, the right way.

As humans, we have the capacity to look deep within ourselves and see what dominates our heart. We are free to invite in other powers to help us reshape our ultimate concern or to chose a more attractive one,

one that will give us greater hope for a better existence and dignify our days. You can make yourself your own worst enemy by not using this important human capability and by allowing second-rate matters to dominate your ambitions and shape your choices and actions.

The Destructiveness of Indifference

While driving to another part of town recently, we passed by a worksite where a crew was repairing a downed power line. As our car crept past the scene, we could not help noticing that several of the utility company's employees were standing around doing nothing. So, too, were a number of police officers who were on the scene. It was impossible for us to understand why four police cruisers—their engines running and lights flashing—were needed when the utility company had the problem under control. In fact, it was their employees who directed the traffic. Perhaps the reason why those half dozen or more persons, who were on one payroll or another, stood around doing nothing in particular was that they were enjoying the moment of not working. But these unproductive people were also showing something else by their actions: indifference to what they should be doing, to their work responsibilities.

Look around and you might find a few people who are dominated by negative qualities—things like meanness, destructiveness, selfishness, and other evils of many sorts. You might also be aware of other lives that are guided and uplifted by the highest hopes and ideals civilization has known: love, justice, truth, pursuit of holiness. But between these two extremes—between those whose hearts are dominated by the worst sorts of qualities and those whose hearts are dominated by the best sorts of qualities—is to be found one of the most pathetic states known to the human condition. These are lives that have no greater purpose than the pursuit of happiness. This widespread aim inevitably leads a person to the state of littleness. There are many otherwise decent and potentially productive persons who have slipped unknowingly and unintentionally into states of littleness. Littleness results wherever there is indifference—particularly to things large and enduring. The list of things to which one can be indifferent is endless. One can be indifferent to being punctual, to completing assignments in a timely manner, to dressing appropriately for work, to taking directions from higher-ups, to keeping up on the latest technological advancements, to being ethical, to working with others effectively, to being a good team player. In the workplace indifference leads ultimately to ineffectiveness.

Contrast those who are okay with turning out sloppy work and who allow defects to slip past with a cleaning lady I (Charles) observed while walking across our campus recently. Her job was to clean bathrooms, to dust furniture, and vacuum floors. But she took pride in the building in which she worked and since leaves had begun to fall from surrounding trees, she saw something that needed her loving touch. So, here she was, giving an extra effort, sweeping leaves off the steps and walkway around the building in which she worked. It wasn't her job but it was something she thought needed doing. So she did it. As I walked past her I sensed in her a certain enthusiasm, a feeling that she really cared more about keeping those steps cleared of leaves and looking nice than she did about her own comfort—for it was cold and crisp that morning. In her mind, I believe, work gave her a chance to care about something. To her, work wasn't a form of drudgery to have to put up with. It was an opportunity to serve. This cleaning woman's example gives us an excellent pattern to follow if we want to escape the trap of littleness. It is to care about doing something that matters.

When one traces to its source the secret of the big life, he is led back to the inner chambers of the human heart, where he finds dwelling a dominating desire, an ultimate concern, for something large and useful—the Good. The "Good" is a philosophical term, meaning that which ennobles the human condition, and there are endless possibilities for heightening the quality of life by pursuing the ideal of the good: amicable working relationships, safe working conditions, eradication of abuse and mistreatment of people, meaningful work, scientific and technological advancements, quality products and services that consumers value and find enjoyable, profitable enterprise that rewards employees monetarily and pays its fair share of taxes.

One of the worst things about indifference is that it makes the human being inhuman. It is far more dangerous than anger and hatred. Anger can lead to creativity. Many new ideas, novel artistic expressions, and movements to remedy wrongs have grown out of anger. Hatred, too, can bring response—people fight it, they denounce it, they disarm it. But "indifference," as Elie Wiesel, who was awarded the Nobel Prize for peace in 1986, said, "means 'no difference.' A strange and unnatural state in which the lines blur between light and darkness, dusk and dawn, crime and punishment, cruelty and compassion, good and evil." Indifference is tempting, even seductive. Humans show their indifference when they look the other way, choose not to try to right a wrong, come to the aid of victims. As Elie Wiesel once said in a speech, "It is much easier to avoid such rude interruptions to our work, our dreams, our hopes. For the person who is indifferent, his or her neighbors are of no consequence. And, therefore, their lives are meaningless. Their hidden or even visible anguish is of no interest. Indifference reduces the other person to an abstraction. Indifference, then, is not only a sin, it is a punishment."

Wiesel recalls the day when, as a young Jewish boy, American soldiers liberated him and others from a Nazi concentration camp, Buchenwald. He remembers their rage at what they saw. He will always be grateful to them for that rage and for their compassion. This is what's possible when people have an ultimate concern that pulls them out of indifference. They have the capacity to be sickened by what they see—they are made human by their capacity to care, to feel rage.

Anyone who works in a private enterprise knows how easy it is to become so concerned with the bottom line that those who work to make profitable results possible in the first place get neglected, their interests ignored. In these circumstances, people are not seen as people but as abstractions—a cost element necessary for work to be performed. When concern for making the numbers outweighs everything else, those who perform day-to-day operations are invariably treated horribly. You can always tell the caliber of a person by what it is that makes them angry. Let us tell you about an incident that demonstrates this.

In Chicago many years ago a man named Paul Galvin had a very good idea—and he made it work. Paul saw a possibility of putting radios into cars; and the radios his company made became popular selling points for many automobiles. Maybe you have heard of his company, Motorola. Today they make cell phones and other kinds of technology-based products. But what's more interesting is how Paul thought of his employees. One day while he was visiting one of his plants he noticed a group of women working on a production line. That wasn't so unusual. But what caught Paul's attention was that these women were bundled up in overcoats trying to keep out the cold. He asked the shop foreman, "Why?" The answer: because they were running production on a single line and the remainder of the shop was idle, they were cutting costs by conserving fuel and heat. Paul Galvin was outraged and reacted sternly: "I don't care if there is one woman working, or ten, or one hundred. You treat them all alike and don't save money by abusing anyone."

Be in Awe of Powers and Ideals Greater than Your Self

Harry Emerson Fosdick captured a penetrating insight into the human predicament when he observed that a person's thoughts can be focused in three different directions—down, out, and up. "He can look down on things and animals beneath him in the scale of life; he can look out at comrades of his own humankind, upon a level with him; but he has also this other faculty from which the finest elements in human life have sprung—he can look up." The trouble with many people, said Fosdick, is that they try to base their lives on the first two capacities without the third. They master the elements below them; they live amicably with their companions and associates. They fail to grasp the fact that the greatest things humans do spring not from the things they command, but from the things they reverence; not from the lowest elements that serve them but from the Highest whom they serve.

Being in awe of things greater than self enables a person to have the "right feelings" when these are the right feelings to have. Consider the woman who regards right and wrong as being terribly important. She is, thereby, able to feel shame and admit that she is wrong, ask forgiveness, and work to restore relationships when she realizes she has acted despicably. The man who values the dignity of others is able to put his pride in its proper place and ask himself what he has been doing lately to be an unbearable bore and nuisance to others.

By humbling oneself to higher values and standards, anyone can grow richer and deeper as a human being. One of our friends told of a time when a colleague witnessed an emotionally wrenching encounter between a supervisor and a subordinate. The boss scolded a newcomer publicly. He was unusually harsh in his criticisms of the employee and he cursed at her. A coworker who witnessed the incident felt sickened and the more she reflected on the incident the sicker she felt inside. In fact, she trembled. So, courageously, the upset bystander went to the abusive boss later in the day and confronted him. She expressed how upset his actions had made her feel. To his credit, the boss listened. Shortly afterward, the boss went to the employee he had scolded and apologized for his temper-filled outburst. He also apologized to the witness he had upset. The boss recognized he had done something wrong and acted to mend the damage he caused.

Two of the deadliest inhibitors of a person's capacity to be in awe of the ideals that dignify life are pride and the inability to see the unseen. Why is pride harmful? In every human life there is a mysterious urge, an inner desire to control one's self. This desire can be both a blessing and a curse. On the one hand this desire has led humans toward an understanding of their universe and how to make their lives in it better, more comfortable, more meaningful, more human. On the other hand this desire has also sometimes led humans to feel that they are the ultimate power in the universe. Something in our human nature calls us to try to control our planet and all that goes on in it. But when we do we also become vulnerable to believing that we are the only force that is capable of control and the only power in control.

Afflicted with this kind of pride, humans begin to think that they are also wise enough to make up the rules and have the final say. This is the worst kind of pride. It involves believing that nothing greater than ourselves exists. It deceives people into believing that nothing is so important as their own safety, comfort, and material well-being. This kind of pride makes a person incapable of seeing anything beyond self. It leads a person to believe that the ultimate in intelligence is human intelligence, that the greatest creative ability is human creative ability, and that the finest artistic expression comes from human minds. This kind of pride leads humans to feel that they alone define what constitutes good and evil and they alone are the ones to make the final judgments on what is right or wrong, good or bad.

A good way to escape many self-inflicted difficulties is to rise above pride. A prideful person is incapable of being in awe of those whose talents and accomplishments surpass theirs. They are incapable of improving themselves by seeing how they might be better performers. Here is a simple illustration of what we mean. In his biography, the great flautist, Jean-Pierre Rampal, wrote that young people, particularly Americans, have a hard time with criticism. They tend to feel that they are an equal with even the greatest of the masters. As it is with others known to be among the finest performers in their respective fields, the source of Rampal's greatness does not reside alone in his innate talents. Rather, its source is his choosing to be in awe of the ungraspable ideals of musical expression, the perfection of the aesthetic.

This same awe shapes also how he sees his role as teacher. The most important role of any teacher is to get students to be in awe of greatness, not themselves. To this end, Rampal is brutally honest, not just with himself but also with others. "The most important criterion for any teacher is honesty," said the great flautist. "It's necessary to say what you believe is true about the way a student plays. For some people," says Rampal, "this is a bitter pill to swallow."

One day a young American girl came to Rampal for a lesson. He asked to hear what she had prepared to play. After a few measures, the master stopped her. He tried to explain that she played the music badly; she needed to work harder. "My dear, the sound isn't good, the technique is faulty and what you played sounded bad," he told her. With tears in her eyes, the flustered girl protested: "No one has ever spoken to me like that before." Her response carried the implication—how dare you! Rampal told her that he didn't want to hurt her feelings but he wasn't about to lie to her. "What good would it be to say *'bravo, c'est magnifique!'* when the whole class can hear that you play badly?"

Don't Self-Destruct by Scorning Others

If a person feels superior to others, that person may come to think it is okay to make belittling remarks or caustic comments to them. To the person who scorns others, nothing is off limits. If one can get a laugh or derive a feeling of superiority by degrading another's dignity, then do it—that's the nature of mockery. Anything can be ridiculed. Anything can be exploited for a cheap laugh. Anything can be taken down. Nothing is sacred. Tom once published a story that recalled an event in his boyhood—when he was sure of his strength and sensed it had no limit. It illustrates, in epitome, the attitude of mockery and how foolish it is to mock what ought never to be ridiculed.

> My parents took my sister and me to the Portland (Oregon) zoo, which was then a modest little park, with several dozen caged animals displayed for the entertainment of the public. One of the cages held a scruffy brownish-yellow male lion, an animal who bore no resemblance to the King of the Beasts and snored more than he roared. My sister and I dubbed him the Sleepy Lion and would shout at him through the cage to wake up and amuse us.

I don't know what possessed me that day to torment the beast. Egged on by my sister, I put my head through the bars of the lion's cage and waited for him to open his eyes. I stared directly into his eyes. My eyes on his eyes, his eyes looking away from mine, avoiding my stare. Fully awake, rising to his feet, the lion walked to the other side of the cage. I followed him. He looked back at me. I stared him in the face. He looked away. I heard a soft growl. I walked alongside him from one side of the cage to the other, fixing him with my stare. Minutes passed. My sister had left to join our parents at the picnic table.

I was alone with the lion. I stared and stared into his face. He looked back at me straight in the face. For a second I lost my concentration and thought of something. I don't know what. I looked away. In that second, that split-second that I looked away—I didn't realize I was pressing so close to the bars—the lion, with a ferocity which has caused me to shudder years later, threw his great brown-yellowish body against the metal cage, locked his teeth into the bars, and with one outstretched paw strained mightily through the bars to tear at me.

Stunned, I recoiled in cold sweat fear. I could not stay. I didn't want to leave. I felt small, humiliated, ashamed of myself. I had offended the beast as if I had offended God with my sin. I had gone beyond the limit. Foolishly I supposed I could impose on this powerful and mysterious beast my childhood games.

A good way to advance your standing in the eyes of others and develop effective working relationships with others is to curb your arrogance—any feeling that you are better than others. Born of pride, scornful ridicule of others, of established standards and values usually invites self-defeating troubles. What Tom did as a small boy with a caged lion, many adults do to others in their organization and to their competitors. What makes these actions self-defeating is that they crowd out better actions, actions that could actually lead to progress in the form of better product, improved service, and more effective interpersonal relationships. Any time a person tries to set himself above others—this is what one does in mocking others—that person sets himself apart from them too. It is difficult to work effectively with such people.

In debates and heated exchanges it is very tempting to say things that have truth to them but which are also hurtful and uncivil. These comments may be highly satisfying and amusing. They can even provide others with a source of laughter. But these same comments may also reveal a certain level of deeper meanness in the person who blurted them out. Another surefire way of creating a negative impression and alienating yourself from others is by being an overly aggressive critic. Practically every group or organization is plagued with a person who feels it is his or her duty to criticize others and practically everything else that goes on. In meetings, for example, this type has a way of pinpointing every possible flaw or shortcoming in what another person says or presents as a suggestion. Instead of working together with others toward the larger purpose, the self-appointed critic focuses attention on humiliating coworkers—perhaps the critic enjoys doing this. It isn't that the critic dislikes others; it's that he or she seems to find enjoyment from coming off as superior to them.

Here is some practical advice that can help you defeat self-destructive pride: any time you find yourself speaking scornfully of someone or something else, ask yourself, "Is this the best use of my time? Am I making it harder for myself to work with this other person? Couldn't I be doing something else that would bring me a better return?" One specific way of not falling into the habit of being an annoying critic is to focus on the good aspects of other people's suggestions. In this way, you can encourage the better-quality thinking that you desire and win the favorable opinion of those around you.

Seeing the Unseen

Another inhibitor of one's ability to be in awe of powers and ideals greater than self is the inability to see the unseen. Our materialistic world is doing its best to convince us that the only realities are those that we can see and touch. If you cannot measure it, the realists believe, then, it isn't important. Perhaps part of the reason for these tendencies—to not see the unseen—is that in modern societies humans are becoming increasingly cut off from the natural world. Whereas in earlier times they were able to witness nature's miracles—birth, change, death, rebirth—now all they know is manicured lawns, house pets, paved streets, skyscrapers, and electronic gadgetry. Isolated from the mysteries of life on our planet, humans begin to feel that they themselves are the ultimate cause of what happens. For them, reality becomes what one can see and touch—what others have made.

There are no mysteries to behold beyond what humans themselves have created. For urban dwellers in particular, almost everything they come into contact with has been made by humans. Nature is distant, not experienced firsthand. And when it is, it is usually seen as some kind of toy to be used for amusement or conquered, as recreational enthusiasts scale rocks, ride about in their all-terrain vehicles, and run river rapids on float boats. For many urban dwellers, nature is something they may experience by watching television programs. All that's important to them are the tangibles. Having a sense of awe for things like truth, beauty, justice, goodness, God—the ideals and powers that ennoble the quality of life on our planet—is lost. The sad reality is that it is the ability to see the unseen that gives human life meaning and dignity.

Consider the situation where a sales manager tells a friend about a move she is about to make to a better position in another part of the country. She talks about the higher level she will fill in the organization. She describes the office complex she will work in and its convenience to where she will be living. She mentions the size of her budget and her expense account. These are purposes for which she has worked. But what she does not consider are the nonmaterial possibilities of the new situation, possibilities that could provide her with a lasting sense of significance: how she will be in a position to improve customer service, improve the working lives of employees, launch better products. Another illustration of the inability to see the unseen arises almost every spring when the National Football League drafts college players—a few of those drafted have one or more years of college eligibility left to play. Notice the comments you hear people make about these players: "He's smart to accept the professional contract. With all the money he'll get, he'll have no more worries." Those who say such things demonstrate a certain kind of blindness. They are unable to see the value of things unseen: education, intellectual and spiritual fulfillment, making oneself a more complete person.

Think of Work as an Opportunity to Serve

The idea of service offers extraordinary possibilities for anyone. Viewing your work as a chance to serve others can enable you to perform exceptionally well and derive enormous personal satisfaction from what you do. Let us begin our explanation of this idea by recounting a simple, yet most revealing incident we observed in a café in Oregon. There we noticed a young woman working as a server. After bringing an order to customers at one table she went into another part of the dining area where she cleared another table. After wiping the surface with a damp towel, she bent over and sighted across the table's surface. The sunlight danced off the table top, showing it to be completely clean—all except for one small spot, which she rubbed away at further to remove a stubborn residue. Now the table was cleaned to her satisfaction. Surely, this young woman's ultimate concern extended far deeper than clean tables. But if one were to peer more deeply into her heart, one would find that she wasn't concerned at all with what she would be getting. Instead, she was focused on giving—she wanted to make sure that the table on which she would serve her next customers was absolutely spotless.

If you want to improve your performance, elevate your image, and derive increased satisfaction from what you do, try taking a service approach in what you do at work. We have witnessed countless examples of ordinary men and women who have produced remarkable results not in just their performance but in themselves as human beings through serving. Working with a service-minded attitude can usually change anyone—dramatically and for the better.

Nathan Ancell, the man who with his brother-in-law started and ran the Ethan Allen Furniture Company for many years, explained the phenomenon we are examining this way. "Human nature," Ancell said, "is controlled by the law of self-preservation, which leads to a feeling that you should take care of yourself first, and take care of feathering your own nest first, and you don't think of taking care of somebody else first. But that's the way most people function and that's why most people fail at becoming successful, because they put their priorities backwards." We would like to point to one more piece of evidence that supports the truth of this philosophy. All over the world business people in their local communities meet once each week for fellowship. These are the men and women who own and operate the successful businesses in their communities. They are also the doctors, lawyers, judges, and police chiefs that serve and protect. They are the members of Rotary International. What's Rotary's slogan? It is this: "He profits most who serves best."

Why does service lead to a better world and to a better life than the pursuit of being served? To answer that, let's consider what selfless service demands of those who choose to follow that path. Living to serve demands a radical departure from customary attitudes, orientations, and habit patterns. It requires boldness to put oneself second and something greater first. It requires vigilance to monitor one's feelings and actions to maintain these priorities. And it requires a person to hold his or her pride in check and to not feel too smug, or proud or self-righteous for what has been accomplished.

Service—we are talking about genuine, authentic service—demands three things of a person. Each one is a challenge, yet each is essential. An authentic service-oriented approach to work calls individuals to (1) obliterate oneself as the central focus of concern, (2) make whatever sacrifices are necessary to shoulder the responsibilities and carry out the work to be done cheerfully, and (3) never seek praise, sympathy, or expect rewards, but to serve with an authentic attitude of helpfulness and goodwill. If you follow these steps faithfully, after a while you will change. In fact, once you acquire this pattern and it becomes natural, you may never want to change back to the way you once were.

Help Make Your Boss Look Good

One of the most practical suggestions we can make that will help anyone succeed is this: act in ways that make life easier for your boss. Help your boss to look good by doing your job especially well and by contributing more than is asked or expected of you—in a word, "overdeliver." In a world in which we measure success primarily by what we get and where we are inclined to give our efforts grudgingly unless we are assured of a payoff to ourselves, going above the call of duty is rare. When the idea of work becomes purely an economic exchange in a person's mind, something terribly limiting happens. That person cripples his or her ability to serve, to make life easier for those higher up in the chain of command. Gone is the joy that could come from being generous and giving of oneself to a worthy cause—the success of an enterprise that does good things.

A man we know named Bill owns and runs a company that sells and installs office furniture for businesses in San Francisco. When he was just getting started and in need of all the sales he could get, a friend introduced Bill to a potential client. Bill's firm won the contract, and it was a big one, worth about $1 million. All seemed to be going well until it was learned that a shipment of new office furniture that had been ordered from a manufacturer back east was lost. The manufacturer had no idea where the truck carrying the load of furniture was—they had contracted with an independent trucker to haul the load. One of Bill's key employees, his service manager, went to work on the problem. She telephoned everyone who might be of assistance. After learning what the trucker's route was, she began tracing all possible leads—had this truck been in an accident? By checking with local police and state highway patrol records she made a breakthrough. It turned out that the truck driver had a small business of his own on the side. In the middle of a Midwestern cornfield this driver was growing marijuana. The police got wind of it and arrested him when he stopped his truck (loaded with the furniture order headed to San Francisco) to check on his illegal crop. The truck was now sitting by the side of a country road not going anywhere, its driver behind bars in a local jail. Bill's service manager contacted the manufacturer, who arranged for another independent driver to transport the load to the west coast. She thereby made her boss look good to his client.

Helping Others Generously

The glory of living is not found by grasping for and clinging to things and saving oneself from hardships, but by spending one's days doing what's truly worthwhile. The trick is to spend one's days wisely. It is a sad day when a person knows what ought to be done but has not the will to do it. The clock ticks, time passes, days turn into months, months into years. Before long, life on earth has ended. To delay doing is to destroy—it is to destroy one's self. Holding on to one's old ways where the self is center stage—a demanding mouth to feed and a frozen heart with an insatiable appetite for things—is a form of self-destruction. There is much to be said for acting immediately, while it is day and one is free to act.

There is just one way to learn how to serve, and that is by serving. Generosity is not a quality humans are born with. It must be learned, and learning it involves acting in generous ways. When one serves with a generous spirit, the value of service becomes apparent. In some families youngsters are taught to be service-minded not by the lectures but by the deeds of their elders. Irving Stone, who headed American Greetings, the firm his father started in Cleveland, told me of how he learned the lessons of service. "Our family was brought up with the belief we ought to help take care of our neighbors. I remember in 1918, there was an influenza epidemic. My grandmother was making soup. All the neighbors were sick. I was a kid, nine years old, taking pots of soup to everyone. We were drilled with that sort of belief. You don't live for yourself."

We generally most admire and most willingly follow those who are genuinely concerned about others. It isn't that we like them because we get something from them. We value the persons they are as a result of their generous nature. Their generosity permeates their every action. By serving without expecting praise or reward, humbly, genuinely, anonymously, a person escapes the ever-present ego-driven desire for praise. When you learn to let go of what you cling to now and become generous and service-minded in all you do, especially in your everyday work duties, you will find yourself saying "yes" to life and derive the highest form of satisfaction.

Have you heard the name Rockefeller? Sure you have. Who hasn't? But there is one incredibly important fact that you might not know about this man, John D. Rockefeller, the very Gibraltar of capitalism. While in his teens, in Cleveland, Rockefeller worked in a commercial house and attended Folsom's Commercial College. Each month, from his weekly earnings of $3.50, he contributed $1.80 for religious purposes, which included his Baptist Sunday school and the Five Points Mission in New York slums. Through summer and winters young Rockefeller wore the same shabby coat; his contributions continued.

Perhaps the finest thing you can do in life is to set a good example for others to follow. This is what we call the contagion of goodness. Here is an example. Many years ago, a young man working for a large corporation was distraught. His wife was diagnosed with incurable cancer. They had four children, ranging in age from six months to seven years. His company's medical coverage was inadequate to cover the expenses he would incur to care for his children and pay his wife's medical bills. One day the young man got a call. A senior vice president and director of the company asked him to come to his office after work. The young man went there. He sat down. A few words were spoken. Then the vice president pushed an envelope across his desk toward the young man and said, "I put some cash in there. You know I make a hell of a lot more money than you do. I don't want you to sign a note. If you ever get in a position at some point where you can repay it or do the same thing for somebody else, you do that. I don't want any obligation, but I want you to use it for the benefit of your wife and kids. And I don't want you to have any worries about it because I'm never going to miss it."

Many years later the man whose wife died of cancer was in a position to do the same kind thing for another person who was going through what he had experienced years before. And he did, because he remembered how grateful he was when someone helped him out when he was going through tough times. Good produces more good, it's contagious.

We caution you that doing fine things for others always has a negative possibility associated with it. That negative possibility is what we talked about at the beginning of this chapter, the feeling of pride. It is a smug, self-righteous feeling that can attack you immediately after you have just done something good. Knowing that you have done something good brings a feeling that you are slightly superior to others because of what you have just done. Resist this temptation. It is pride acting in its destructive way. Pride generally attacks us when we are at our best because it is at these moments that we are most vulnerable to its seductive powers. A woman does a fine and generous thing. That's good. But knowing what she just did, she is tempted to feel she is a little bit better than the next person. This is bad. It's destructive because pride can cause anyone to do good things for the wrong reasons—to expect praise from others, to feel good about oneself, to think of oneself as better than others, especially those helped or served. The person who acts generously while selfishly expecting rewards in return may get those rewards immediately but that's all this person will receive. Most times these types are exposed for what they really are, self-serving phonies. The wisdom of our ancestors tells us this: it is a mistake to be disingenuous in serving others. It must be authentic.

Being generous involves far more than just being charitable. It ought to be thought of as a state of mind, an orientation to all that one does at work. A generous person is a "giving person," a person who is more interested in serving others and seeing to it that they are made better off. A man we know named Walter, who recently retired as national sales manager for a well-known company that makes and sells cardboard containers, told us of a situation he once faced that was made better because of his generosity. One Sunday afternoon, Walter received a frantic phone call from one of his valued customers. The customer told him that his firm faced a severe problem. They had just learned from warehouse personnel that they were woefully short of cardboard containers. And they needed several hundred dozen to ship an important order to one of their customers. Walter's generous nature responded. He told his customer, "Don't worry. I will personally see to it that you will have those boxes tomorrow morning." This would require special effort, because the warehouse containing the cardboard boxes Walter's company sold was closed—no personnel were working there that day.

After hanging up the telephone, Walter called one of his managers. "Meet me at the warehouse in fifteen minutes," he told him. Once at the warehouse, Walter got to work. He located the needed containers, got into a forklift truck and began loading them onto a truck. It took several hours but between Walter and his manager, they got the needed containers loaded and sent on their way in time for the promised delivery. More interested in serving than snoozing that afternoon, Walter and his manager made a good customer into a very loyal and thankful customer. Now the next time this customer's company is receiving bids for cardboard containers, do you think price will matter all that much?

Be generous. Pass your generosity on to others so they can receive the gift of being service-minded and generous themselves. You'll never miss what you give away in time, possessions, or efforts. When you do you these things—when you serve others authentically—you will find happiness, real happiness.

BIBLIOGRAPHY

Acuff, Jerry and Wally Wood. *The Relationship Edge in Business: Connecting with Customers and Colleagues When It Counts.* New York: Wiley, 2004.

Allport, Gordon W. *The Individual and His Religion: A Psychological Interpretation.* New York: Macmillan, 1959.

Baldwin, Neil. *Edison: Inventing the Century.* New York: Hyperion, 1995.

Bandura, Albert. *Self-Efficacy: The Exercise of Control.* New York: W. H. Freeman, 1997.

Branden, Nathaniel. *How to Raise Your Self-Esteem.* New York: Bantam, 1987.

———. *The Six Pillars of Self-Esteem.* New York: Bantam, 1994.

———. *Taking Responsibility.* New York: Fireside, 1997.

Byron, William J., S. J. *Jesuit Saturdays: Sharing the Ignatian Spirit with Lay Colleagues and Friends.* Chicago: Loyola Press, 2000.

Cameron, Julia. *The Artist's Way: A Spiritual Path to Higher Creativity.* New York: Tarcher/Putnam, 1992.

Carter, John Mack and Joan Feeney (compilers). *Starting at the Top: America's New Achievers: Twenty Three Success Stories Told by Men and Women Whose Dreams of Being Boss Came True.* New York: Morrow, 1985.

Chesbrough, Henry W. *The New Imperative for Creating and Profiting from Technology.* Boston: Harvard Business School Press, 2003.

Cudney, Milton R. and Robert E. Hardy. *Self-Defeating Behaviors: Free Yourself from the Habits, Compulsions, Feelings, and Attitudes that Hold You Back.* San Francisco: HarperSanFrancisco, 1993.

Demarais, Ann and Valerie White. *First Impressions: What You Don't Know About How Others See You.* New York: Bantam, 2004.

Ellis, Albert. *Overcoming Procrastination.* New York: New American Library, 1979.

Feinberg, Mortimer and John J. Tarrant. *Why Smart People Do Dumb Things.* New York: Fireside, 1995.

Forni, P.M. *Choosing Civility: The Twenty Five Rules of Considerate Conduct.* New York: St. Martin's Press, 2002.

Fosdick, Harry Emerson. *Twelve Tests of Character.* New York: Association Press, 1923.

Frank, George. *Adventures in Wood Finishing: 88 Rue De Charonne.* Newton, CT: Taunton Press, 1981.

Garvin, David A. *Learning in Action: A Guide to Putting the Learning Organization to Work.* Boston: Harvard Business School Press, 2000.

Gladwell, Malcolm. *Blink: The Power of Thinking without Thinking.* Boston: Little, Brown, 2005.

Gomersall, Earl R. and M. Scott Myers. "Breakthrough in On-the-Job Training." *Harvard Business Review,* July–August, 1966, pp. 62–72.

Goulston, Mark. *Get Out of Your Own Way at Work . . . and Help Others Do the Same: Conquering Self-Defeating Behavior on the Job.* New York: Putnam Adult, 2005.

Govindarajan, Vijay and Chris Trimble. *Ten Rules for Strategic Innovation: From Idea to Execution.* Boston: Harvard Business School Press, 2005.

Harman, Willis W. and Howard Rheingold. *Higher Creativity: Liberating the Unconscious for Breakthrough Insights.* Institute of Noetic Sciences. Los Angeles: J. P. Tarcher, 1984.

Herodotus. *Persian Wars,* Book 1 of *The Complete and Unabridged Historical Works of Herodotus.* Edited by Francis Godolphin and Richard Borroum. New York: Random House, 1942.

Hocking, William Ernest. *Human Nature and Its Remaking.* New Haven: Yale University Press, 1923.

Idinopulos, Thomas A. *The Erosion of Faith.* Chicago: Quadrangle Books, 1971.

Israel, Paul. *Edison: A Life of Invention.* New York: Wiley, 1998.

Kilpatrick, William Kirk. *Psychological Seduction: The Failure of Modern Psychology.* Nashville, TN: Thomas Nelson, 1983.

Leary, Mark R. *Self Presentation: Impression Management and Interpersonal Behavior.* Madison, WI: Brown & Benchmark, 1995.

McGregor, Jena. "How Failure Breeds Success." *Business Week,* July 10, 2006, 42–52.

McLean, Bethany and Peter Elkind. *The Smartest Guys in the Room: The Amazing Rise and Sacanalous Fall of Enron.* New York: Penguin, 2003.

McNichols, Thomas J. *The Case of the Missing Time*. Boston: Harvard Business School Press (KEL071), 1973.

Mitchell, Mary. *The First Five Minutes: How to Make a Great First Impression in Any Business Situation*. New York: Wiley, 1998.

Naumann, Earl. "10 Easy Ways to Lose Customer Trust." *Business Horizons*, September/October 1992, 30–34.

Nelson, Bob. *1001 Ways to Take Initiative at Work*. New York: Workman, 1999.

Noles, Randy. *Orange Blossom Boys: The Untold Story of Ervin T. Rouse, Chubby Wise and the World's Most Famous Fiddle Tune*. Anaheim, CA: Centerstream Publications, 2002.

OSHA. gov/oshDoc/toc_FatalFacts.html.

Peale, Cliff. "Secretary Works Her Way to Head Sweco." *Cincinnati Enquirer*, June 8, 2006, A 14–15.

Plutarch. "Solon," in *The Lives of the Noble Grecians and Romans*. Translated by John Dryden and revised by Arthur Clough. New York: Modern Library, undated.

Rampal, Jean-Pierre and Deborah Wise Rampal. *Music, My Love: An Autobiography*. New York: Random House, 1989.

Robinson, Alan G. and Sam Stern. *Corporate Creativity: How Innovation and Improvement Actually Happen*. San Francisco: Berrett-Koehler, 1997.

Schwartz, Evan I. *Juice: The Creative Fuel That Drives World-Class Inventors*. Boston: Harvard Business School Press, 2004.

Steel, Piers. "The Nature of Procrastination: A Meta-Analytic and Theoretical Review of Self-Regulatory Failure." *Psychological Bulletin*, 133(1), 2007, 65–94.

Sternberg, Robert J., Editor. *Why Smart People Can Be So Dumb*. New Haven, CT: Yale University Press, 2002.

Stipp, David. "How Disease Evolves." *Fortune*, May 16, 2005, 53–54.

Tillich, Paul. *Dynamics of Faith*. New York: Harper & Row, 1957.

Torrance, E. Paul. *Guiding Creative Talent*. Englewood Cliffs, NJ: Prentice-Hall, 1962.

Trueblood, D. Elton. *The Life We Prize*. New York: Harper, 1951.

Twenge, Jean M. *Generation Me: Why Today's Young Americans Are More Confident, Assertive, Entitled—and More Miserable than Ever Before*. New York: Free Press, 2006.

"UNC Reserve Punter Arrested for Allegedly Stabbing a Rival in Kicking Leg." *USA Today*, September 13, 2006.

United Parcel Service. *J. E. Casey, Our Partnership Legacy*. Greenwich, CT: UPS, 1985.

Vardy, Peter. *Being Human: Fulfilling Genetic and Spiritual Potential.* London: Darton, Longman and Todd, Ltd., 2003.

Wallas, Graham. *The Art of Thought.* New York: Harcourt, Brace & Co., 1926.

Warner, Melanie. "Exorcism at Tyco." *Fortune*, April 28, 2003, 106–108, 110.

Watson, Charles E. *Management Development through Training.* Reading, MA: Addison-Wesley, 1979.

Welch, Jack and Suzy. "Ideas the Welch Way." *Business Week*, June 19, 2006, 100.

White, John. *Rejection.* Reading, MA: Addison-Wesley, 1982.

Wind, Jerry, Colin Crook, and Robert Gunther. *The Power of Impossible Thinking: Transform the Business of Your Life and the Life of Your Business.* Philadelphia, PA: Wharton School Publishing, 2006.

Woodruff, Paul. *Reverence: Renewing a Forgotten Virtue.* New York: Oxford University Press, 2001.

Young, Steve. *Great Failures of the Extremely Successful: Mistakes, Adversity, Failure and Other Steppingstones to Success.* Los Angeles: Tallfellow Press, 2004.

INDEX

About the Authors

CHARLES E. WATSON is Professor of Management at Miami University (Ohio). A former manager with wide business experience, he is the author of over two dozen articles and eight books on management, including *Managing with Integrity* (Praeger, 1991; a Book-of-the-Month Club selection) and *How Honesty Pays* (Praeger, 2005).

THOMAS A. IDINOPULOS is Professor of Comparative Religions at Miami University (Ohio). The author of many books, he has also published more than eighty-five articles on religion, politics, and literature in such publications as the *Journal of Religion*, *Scottish Journal of Theology*, and *Journal of the American Academy of Religion*.